CAMBRIDGE STUDIES IN LINGUISTICS

General Editors: B. COMRIE, C. J. FILLMORE, R. HUDDLESTON, R. LASS, D. LIGHTFOOT, J. LYONS, P. H. MATTHEWS, R. POSNER, S. ROMAINE, N. V. SMITH, N. VINCENT

From etymology to pragmatics

In this series

Supplementary volumes

Earlier issues not listed are also available
**Issued in hardback and paperback*

FROM ETYMOLOGY TO PRAGMATICS

Metaphorical and cultural aspects of semantic structure

EVE SWEETSER

Department of Linguistics
University of California at Berkeley

CAMBRIDGE
UNIVERSITY PRESS

PUBLISHED BY THE PRESS SYNDICATE OF THE UNIVERSITY OF CAMBRIDGE
The Pitt Building, Trumpington Street, Cambridge CB2 1RP, United Kingdom

CAMBRIDGE UNIVERSITY PRESS
The Edinburgh Building, Cambridge CB2 2RU, UK http://www.cup.cam.ac.uk
40 West 20th Street, New York, NY 10011–4211, USA http://www.cup.org
10 Stamford Road, Oakleigh, Melbourne 3166, Australia

First published 1990
First paperback edition 1991
Reprinted 1993, 1994, 1995, 1997, 1998

Printed in the United Kingdom at the University Press, Cambridge

British Library cataloguing in publication data
Sweetser, Eve
   From etymology to pragmatics. Metaphorical and
   cultural aspects of semantic structure. – (Cambridge
   studies in linguistics; 54)
   1. Linguistics
   I. Title
   410

Library of Congress Cataloguing in Publication data
Sweetser, Eve.
From etymology to pragmatics: metaphorical and cultural aspects
of semantic structure/Eve Sweetser.
   p.   cm. – (Cambridge studies in linguistics; 54)
Bibliography
ISBN 0 521 32406 8
1. Semantics. 2. Grammar, Comparative and general. 3. Modality
(Linguistics) I. Title II. Series.
P325.S96   1990
401'.43 – dc20 89–7320 CIP

ISBN 0 521 32406 8 hardback
ISBN 0 521 42442 9 paperback

UP

In reconstruction we must deal both with forms and with functions. To reconstruct forms alone, without attention to their functional position, is first and foremost to create a hopelessly unrealistic linguistic situation.

Calvert Watkins, Indo-European origins of the Celtic verb, vol I.
The sigmatic aorist

Most of the older morphemic splits – *that* and *that*, *it* and *it*, etc. – were perpetrated on relatively defenseless grammatical morphemes, in order to accommodate some hypothesis about syntax ... But with the advent of generative semantics, other parts of the lexicon have been exposed to attack.

Dwight Bolinger, Meaning and form

In our understanding of language in general, there seems to be a schema for lexicalization the sense of which is that the act of lexicalizing something is the act of presenting it as an established category of human thought. If a lexical item exists, in other words, it must exist as some part of a frame and must correspond to some part of a schema.

Charles Fillmore, Topics in lexical semantics

Contents

Preface

This book owes an immense and obvious debt to the Berkeley linguistic community. The largest debt of all is to my thesis committee: Charles Fillmore, George Lakoff, and Paul Kay. As advisors, and since then as colleagues, they have constantly added to my understanding of language, and have also been frequent sources of moral support and constructive criticism. Among my other teachers at Berkeley, James Matisoff first developed my interest in historical semantics, and Yakov Malkiel and Johanna Nichols gave much insightful commentary on earlier versions of this work. I would also like to thank Elizabeth Closs Traugott for her encouragement, criticism, and the inspiration provided by her work.

Numerous colleagues have given me the benefits of their experience and knowledge in commenting on various parts of this book. I have tried to implement much of their advice, and apologize for any instances where the work has suffered from my refusal to heed them. Chapter 2 has profited from the comments of Gary Holland, Dwight Bolinger, Eric Hamp, Tom Walsh, and Calvert Watkins. For comments on chapter 3 I am indebted to Dwight Bolinger, Julian Boyd, Gilles Fauconnier, Suzanne Fleischman, Julie Gerhardt, Mark Johnson, Annette Karmiloff-Smith, Robin Tolmach Lakoff, Iskendir Savasir, John Searle, Dan Slobin, and Leonard Talmy. Robin Lakoff and Don Forman have both been influential in the development of my understanding of conjunction, as represented in chapters 4 and 5; Jeanne Van Oosten's work on topicality was also helpful in chapter 5. And thanks to the Fulbright Foundation, my Polish colleague Barbara Dancygier has engaged me in a very productive dialogue on the subject of conditionals. Naomi Quinn, Dorothy Holland, and colleagues who participated in the Princeton Conference on Folk Models have given me a more complex understanding of cognitive structures. Mark Johnson and Mark Turner have in different ways deeply shaped my views on metaphor. I learned a great deal about semantic change from exchanges of ideas with Bill Croft, Suzanne Kemmer, and

Nancy Wiegand. Vassiliki Nikiforidou, as my student and office-mate, has been a source of many invaluable insights; and Jane Espenson and Michele Emanatian have both contributed thoughtful commentary. Claudia Brugman and George Lakoff have been kind and astute critics of both content and style, through all the chapters and at all stages of revision: I am deeply grateful to them for this, and even more grateful for their own illuminating work. And Orin Gensler has been inextricably involved in many aspects of this work, as friend, linguistic colleague, stylistic consultant, source of Hebrew data, informant for a useful example, and long-suffering on-line editor of an earlier version.

Cambridge University Press's two readers were very helpful to me. I must in particular thank Professor Frank Palmer for his generous and insightful comments, and even more for his own work on the subject of modality. The patience of my editor, Penny Carter, likewise deserves heartfelt thanks.

The Sloan Foundation, through its support to the Cognitive Science community at Berkeley, gave me access to computer facilities for on-line editing and printing.

I would also like to express my gratitude to Kathryn Klar and Brendan O Hehir, my teachers and colleagues in the area of Celtic linguistics. And among my earlier teachers from Harvard, I acknowledge my debt to Calvert Watkins, Jorge Hankamer, Judith Aissen, and particularly to the wisdom and kindness of the late Cedric Whitman. Among my friends, I especially thank the Uggla family for their friendship and support.

Debts to other members of the scholarly community are readily recognized by other scholars, but the debt of an author to familial support is just as deep, if less tangible. To my parents, who constantly fostered my interest in language, to my siblings and to my husband's family, and most of all to my husband, I can truly say that this book could never have been written without them.

Abbreviations

Br.   Breton
Cl.   Classical
Dan.   Danish
Eng.   English
Fr.   French
Ger.   German
Gk   Greek
Goth.   Gothic
IE   Indo-European
Ir.   Irish
It.   Italian
Lat.   Latin
LGer.   Low German
lit.   literally
MIr.   Middle Irish
Mod.   Modern
NE   New English
OE   Old English
OFr.   Old French
OHG   Old High German
perf.   perfect
Rus.   Russian
Skt   Sanskrit
Sp.   Spanish
Wel.   Welsh

1 *Introduction*

Language is systematically grounded in human cognition, and cognitive linguistics seeks to show exactly how. The conceptual system that emerges from everyday human experience has been shown in recent research to be the basis for natural-language semantics in a wide range of areas.[1] This study will make use of such a cognitive approach to meaning, and show that it can account in a unified fashion for facts in three diverse areas: polysemy; lexical semantic change; and pragmatic ambiguity. All of these areas have in common the fact that they involve one form being used for more than one function. In semantic change, a form historically acquires a new function to replace or augment its old ones; a question which necessarily arises here is what relates the new sense to already extant senses – are there regularities to be observed about the addition of new senses to words, or the loss of older senses? In the case of polysemy (the synchronic linking of multiple related senses to a single form) a parallel question arises: what can we say about the possible groupings of senses to be observed in polysemous words or morphemes – what, for example, differentiates them from the cases of unrelated meanings which share a form (cases which are termed *homonymy* rather than *polysemy*)?[2] In the case of pragmatic ambiguity, a form's basic semantic function is extended pragmatically to cover other referents or meanings: for example, we might say this is the case with a phrase like "How are you?", which arguably retains its original sense as an inquiry about wellbeing, but is also conventionally situationally *interpreted* as a greeting or opener for an encounter. The question in all cases is whether there are regularities to be observed about such mappings of form to multiple functions. I shall be claiming that there are, and that the regularities cannot be appropriately captured within an objectivist semantic theory, wherein meaning is thought of as basically a relationship between word and world – i.e, between a linguistic form and an object or state of affairs referred to or described by that form. However, the observed regularities are natural

1

and readily motivated within a cognitively based theory which takes not the objective "real world," but human perception and understanding of the world to be the basis for the structure of human language.

I shall not primarily be discussing or arguing against specific formal-semantic analyses of polysemy or of meaning change. This may seem surprising to some readers, but it is largely the case that semantic work within the formal-semantic tradition has neglected the study of individual morphemes' meanings in favor of examination of the compositional-semantic structure of larger phrasal and sentential units. Earlier generative work concentrated on the extraction of relevant dimensions of a word's meaning (sometimes called "semantic features") with a view to the observation of what structural contrasts are represented by the vocabulary of a given language (see section 1.1). This approach did not focus on a full, rich understanding of lexical meaning *per se*, but on economical representation of the relevant contrasts. More recently, lexical meaning has been studied largely in the context of compositionality: for example, Dowty (1979), expanding on Vendler (1967), analyzes certain dimensions of the meaning of verb roots, and thereby succeeds in giving a motivated account of the different combinatorial possibilities of the verbs in question. There has also been significant interest in the combinatorial semantics of negation, quantifiers, and adverbs; again, the focus has been on the ways in which syntactic structure affects the relationship of these morphemes to compositional sentence-semantics,[3] rather than on the description of full, rich lexical semantics.[4] Part of the reason for this is probably that the researchers in question expected to find the interesting regularities in the area of compositional sentence-semantics or in the contrasts between word meanings, rather than in the structured interrelationships between senses or uses of a single morpheme.

Generative grammar has rigidly separated synchronic semantic structure from historical change: most formal-semantic analyses to date have thus treated meaning change as inherently irrelevant to analysis of the synchronic system (the latter being the relevant object of study). (Although some of the same attitude once prevailed in structuralist phonology, generative phonology has been more conscious of the need to deal with diachrony than has formal semantics: Kiparsky (1968) is a classic example.) Further, even in a synchronic context, there has, to my knowledge, been little or no attempt in generative grammar to give a principled explanation of polysemy structure. This is particularly odd in view of the fact that Katz and Fodor's original (1963) layout of a plan for feature-semantic analysis of lexical meaning included as a salient example an analysis of the relationship between the different senses of the polysemous word *bachelor* (e.g., "unmarried adult male human, holder of BA degree, junior knight serving another knight ... "). Bolinger's (1965) critique of Katz and Fodor makes it clear that their analysis of *bachelor* has little systematic motivation for its choice of features and their hierarchy, and therefore elucidates little except the authors' intuitions about how the senses might be related. Avoiding the difficulties of motivating one polysemy analysis rather than another, objectivist semantic-feature analyses within this framework have unhesitatingly posited separate lexical items to account for variation in a word's syntactic or semantic behavior, tacitly assuming that these (homonymous?) entities were no more closely connected than if their phonological representations had been unrelated.[5] Such analysts presumably trust that it will be possible to describe and explain meaning-changes or polysemy relations in any successful semantic theory; but the theory is nonetheless constructed without reference to diachrony or polysemy. Although few practicing etymologists would agree that these two areas are unconnected with each other, or that they are unimportant to semantic theory (imagine a theory of phonology which made no systematic effort to deal with the relationship between allophones or to account for observed trends of sound change), nonetheless there exists no fully adequate account either of meaning change or of its relation to polysemy. Recent research in both areas suggests that such an account is best sought for in terms of human cognitive structure.

What we would like to have is a motivated account of the relationships between senses of a single morpheme or word, and of the relationships between historically earlier and later senses of a morpheme or word. By "motivated," I mean an account which appeals to something beyond the linguist's intuition that these senses are related, or that these two senses are more closely related than either is to a third sense. For example, it is possible to crosslinguistically examine meaning changes and to observe what senses frequently historically give rise to what later senses. We would then argue that there is reason to posit a close semantic and cognitive link between two senses if one is regularly a historical source for the other. Or we can examine the polysemy structures of languages, and see what groupings of meanings are regularly found. If a language has (as does English) a *systematic* use of the same vocabulary for root and epistemic modality, we may conclude that, within the language's system, these two classes of senses are closely linked. In section 1.2 I will discuss some of the relatively recent research which has adopted this methodology, and has shown us that it is possible to give serious, well-motivated accounts of the interrelationships of meanings. First I would like to briefly address the question of the cognitive reality of these semantic structural claims.

It should not be a controversial claim that relationships between linguistic form and function reflect human conceptual structure and general principles of cognitive organization. It becomes controversial only in the context of a particular philosophical tradition's understanding of language. Traditional truth-conditional semantic analysis focuses on logical relations such as inference virtually to the exclusion of such linguistic concerns as why the same word might be used to mean very different things. If the meaning of a word or a sentence reduces to a set of conditions which must be met (in the objective real world) for that word to be applicable or for that sentence to be true, then obviously inference (e.g., if these conditions are met, what other conditions do I know must also be met?) is a fruitful area of research, while polysemy is a nearly impenetrable area simply by virtue of the fact that multiple senses of polysemous forms just don't seem to share objective truth-conditions. (For example, there are no necessary *objective* truth-conditions shared between the *see* in *I see the cat on the mat* and *I see what you mean* – the latter can be said equally felicitously by someone wearing a blindfold preventing physical visual perception.) By viewing meaning as the relationship between words and the world, truth-conditional semantics eliminates cognitive organization from the linguistic system. And to a philosopher concerned with abstract truth, the important question is indeed perhaps whether the sort of thing we call "snow" has the color we call "white" in the real world (hence the sentence "Snow is white" will be true rather than false). For the truth of "Snow is white," it may not seem to matter much whether "real world" means an objective world independent of human experience, or an experienced world where *snow* and *white* refer to our experiential classes of objects and colors: in either case, most people are likely to agree on the truth value of the sentence.

But suppose that, instead of *white*, I take Latin *candidus* as my sample word. *Candidus* meant, among other things, "white" and "bright"; but it also meant "open, honest" – as in its English descendent, *candid*. But it seems unlikely that there is any objective correlation in the real world between white things and honest things, or any larger objectively chosen category which includes just these and no others. The "real world," if we

[handwritten margin note: Why does one word have many [?] unrelated meanings?]

mean one which is outside of human cognitive organization, is not so constructed as to group the white with the honest. Rather, it is our cognitive structuring of the world which can create such an identification. And if language uses a word for our cognitive category, then language cannot be described in terms of pure fit between Word and World: unless, by World, we mean our experiential picture of the world.

The choice of which words express which concepts is arbitrary from a truth-conditional point of view. The so-called "arbitrariness of the sign" is a point on which structural linguistics in the Saussurean tradition converges with logical semantics in the Fregean tradition. If all uses of signs are taken as arbitrary, then multiple uses of the same sign must also be seen as arbitrary, and so the relationships between them might be assumed to be uninteresting. Saussure, who was interested in polysemy and in meaning-change, would not himself have taken this simplistic a view. However, it was probably necessary to firmly establish the arbitrary nature of linguistic convention, in order to liberate linguistics from futile attempts to see onomatopoeia at the root of all linguistic usage. We should now be ready to go back to the examination of iconicity and other motivating factors in the choice of linguistic forms, without any danger of losing our understanding of conventionality.

Saussure (1959 [1915]) was right, of course, that there is an essential arbitrary component in the association of words with what they mean. For example, in *I see the tree*, it is an arbitrary fact that the sequence of sounds which we spell *see* (as opposed to the sound sequence spelled *voir* in French) is used in English to refer to vision. But, *given this arbitrary fact*, it is by no means arbitrary that *see* can also mean "know" or "understand," as in *I see what you're getting at*. There is a very good reason why *see* rather than, say, *kick* or *sit*, or some other sensory verb such as *smell*, is used to express knowledge and understanding. Such motivated relationships between word meanings are as much a part of the study of semantics as inference. But the fact that *see* can also mean "know" has little to do with truth conditions; in any objective truth-conditional understanding of vision and knowledge, seeing is accomplished by visual neural response to physical data, while knowing (whatever it may be) has no particular dependence on the visual modality. One sees objects and events; one knows propositions, and not always because of past visual input.

Why then is *see* (as opposed to *kick* or *feel* or *smell*) used to mean knowledge? We are intuitively certain that the choice is not random, that *see* is a well-motivated choice for extension to the sense of knowledge. Our intuition is confirmed by systematic relationships with other lexical items. I will discuss some of these in detail later, but consider the sequence "Do you believe in baptism" "Believe? Hell, I've *seen it!*" If seeing means you *know*, in our understanding of the world, then (since believing is less sure than knowing) it's silly to say we just believe something for which we have direct visual evidence.[6] The answer thus has to do with conceptual organization: it is our understanding that vision and knowledge are related. For this reason, we need a theory of semantics that can take conceptual organization into account.

There are at least two reasons why many theorists have been reluctant to take seriously the idea that language is shaped by cognition. One reason is that linguists have hoped to be able to analyze language relatively independently of the rest of human abilities. I shall return to this issue, but all of the recent research to be discussed in section 1.2, plus examples like *see* and *candidus*, argue that our linguistic system is inextricably interwoven with the rest of our physical and cognitive selves. We can view this with terror at our inability to separate out our data and analyze it as independent of psychology or anthropology. Or we can rejoice in the fact that many aspects of language become much simpler when viewed in the collective light of the human sciences: the study of human culture and cognition is frighteningly broad as a field, but there is no point in pretending the autonomy of language if such a pretense obscures real explanatory possibilities.

The second reason for skepticism is the Sapir–Whorf problem:[7] it may not only be true that our cognitive system shapes our language, but – if such a relationship exists – why not the other direction as well? Perhaps our acquired linguistic categories shape our cognitive system, too. Evidence in this area has tended to be negative. The difference between color-categorization systems in different linguistic communities, for example, was once touted as an example of linguistically based cultural variation, and has now been shown to be a relatively minor and systematic variation, existing against a backdrop of deep similarities. We all *do* see color the same way, whatever words we use for colors, and the possible meanings of color words are limited by our common physical perceptions (Berlin and Kay 1969; Kay and MacDaniel 1978; Kay and Kempton 1984). Analysts of language and culture have become cautious about assuming isomorphism between cognitive and linguistic categories, but particularly about assuming that language shapes culture and cognition (it is hard to deny the converse). The evidence for the shaping of language by human cognition, and *not* the other direction, has been especially convincingly laid out with respect to the vocabulary of physical domains like color and spatial terms. Whether words for cultural categories are merely shaped by our understanding of culture, or whether they shape it as well, is a good deal harder to prove experimentally, since we can't (as was done with colors) assume that the phenomena referred to are the same crosslinguistically.

Perhaps, however, the issue of language shaping cognition is a little less thorny than we thought. For example, few linguists or anthropologists would be upset by the hypothesis that learning a word for a culturally important category could linguistically *reinforce* the learning of the category itself. There seem to be areas, at least, of interdependency between cognition and language. Likewise, it would be hard to deny that much of the basic cognitive apparatus of humans is not dependent on language, and that humans therefore share a great deal of prelinguistic and extralinguistic experience which is likely to shape language rather than to be shaped by it.

Finally, a less naive approach to linguistic structure may obviate some of the objections to claims of cognitive–linguistic interdependency. Suppose, for example, that one language habitually refers to the next week as the week "ahead," while another culture calls it the week "behind." A naive theoretician might put forward a claim, based on this evidence, that the two cultures experienced time differently (see, in fact, Whorf 1956b [1941] for a parallel suggestion about some genuine data). More recent work (see Fillmore 1971; H. Clark 1973) has suggested that languages can choose to lexicalize different ways of thinking about a domain such as time in spatial terms, but that the possible repertory of time vocabularies is nonetheless limited and that the limits are determined by the human perceptual system. The understanding that we have universal, perceptually determined possible options for spatializing time does not eliminate the possibility that strong lexicalization of one option could culturally influence thought patterns. But it does make it clear that the simple presence of divergent ways of talking about time in terms of space (where both ways represent "universal" options) is no argument for equivalent divergence in conceptual patterns.

A naive theoretician might also make the mistake of imagining that some "primitive" culture being studied was *confusing* futurity with physical directionality, in labeling the two concepts identically. But such an analyst would be mistaking metaphoricity for literal usage, a mistake which he or she would readily find the sophistication to avoid in observing an English poem which addressed a lover as "my rose" or "my sun," or even in noticing that English speakers use *see* to mean "know" or "understand."

Taking this slightly more sophisticated viewpoint, it has been argued (Lakoff and Johnson 1980; Johnson 1987; G. Lakoff 1987; Turner 1987) that a great deal of polysemy is due to metaphorical usage, and that in fact not only our language, but our cognition and hence our language, operates metaphorically.[8] If we use a word meaning "white" to mean "honest, candid," rather than using our word for "purple," it is not just a fact about the language. It is a fact about (at least) the cultural community that they see whiteness as metaphorically standing for honesty or moral purity (for example, members of such a society might put on white, rather than red, clothing to ritually indicate purity; this would not be a linguistic convention). The metaphorical use of *white* in English to mean "morally good" (e.g. *white magic* to mean "non-harmful magic") is also part of a broader system; *black magic* is the moral opposite of *white magic*, and *grey* is often used to refer to morally marginal actions. This system of metaphorical uses of color terms is, as mentioned above, not based on a systematic correlation between colors and morality in the world; but it is nonetheless present in speakers' linguistic and cultural models.[9] When a specific linguistic usage, based on such a metaphorical structure, becomes no longer consciously metaphorical (as in "You *see* what I mean?"), then we can say that the linguistic form has acquired a metaphorically motivated secondary sense.

I call this viewpoint sophisticated, because in order to understand metaphor it is necessary to give up our old prejudices: we can no longer insist on a simple relationship between word and world. Looking at speakers with two uses of the same word, we don't have to say either "those two uses refer to the same kind of thing in the real world" or "Those are just separate unrelated uses." We don't even have to say "Speakers *think* those two uses refer to the 'same' kind of thing in the real world." Metaphor allows people to understand one thing as another, without thinking the two things are objectively the same. If knowledge is (as chapter 2 argues in detail) understood partly as seeing, or honesty as whiteness, that by no means indicates that speakers are confusing the source and target domains of these metaphors. (They would not, for example, have any trouble telling the difference between white clothing and candid speech.) A word meaning is not necessarily a group of objectively "same" events or entities; it is a group of events or entities which our cognitive system links in appropriate ways. Linguistic categorization depends not just on our naming of distinctions that exist in the world, but also on our metaphorical and metonymic structuring of our perceptions of the world.

Words do not randomly acquire new senses, then. And since new senses are acquired by cognitive structuring, the multiple synchronic senses of a given word will normally be related to each other in a motivated fashion. By studying the historical development of groups of related words, it should be possible to see what sorts of systematic structure our cognitive system tends to give to the relevant domains. I will begin by applying a cognitive-semantic approach to a well-recognized set of Indo-European etymologies in the hope of explaining a hitherto mysterious fact: certain semantic changes occur over and over again throughout the course of Indo-European and independently in different branches across an area of thousands of miles and a time depth of thousands of years. I will show that a cognitive semantics that allows for metaphorical mapping within the conceptual system can explain such facts straightforwardly, while a truth-conditional approach to semantics cannot.

Synchronic polysemy and historical change of meaning really supply the same data in many ways. No historical shift of meaning can take place without an intervening stage of polysemy. If a word once meant A and now means B, we can be fairly certain that speakers did not just wake up and switch meanings on June 14, 1066. Rather, there was a stage when the word meant both A and B, and the earlier meaning of A eventually was lost. But if an intervening stage of polysemy was involved, then all the historical data, as evidence of past polysemy relations, is an interesting source of information about the reflection of cognitive structure in language. Even more crucially, the historical order in which senses are added to polysemous words tells us something about the directional relationships between senses; it affects our understanding of cognitive structure to know that spatial vocabulary universally acquires temporal meanings rather than the reverse.

The preceding discussion has presupposed that we cannot rigidly separate synchronic from diachronic analysis: all of modern socio-linguistics has confirmed the importance of reuniting the two. As with the language and cognition question, the synchrony/diachrony interrelationship has to be seen in a more sophisticated framework. The structuralist tradition spent considerable effort on eliminating *confusion* between synchronic regularities and diachronic changes: speakers do not necessarily have rules or representations which reflect the language's past history. But neither Saussure nor any of his colleagues would have denied that synchronic structure inevitably reflects its history in important ways: the whole chess metaphor is a perfect example of Saussure's deep awareness of this fact.[10] Saussure, of course, uses chess because for future play the past history of the board is totally irrelevant: you can analyze a chess problem without any information about past moves. But he could hardly have picked – as he must have known – an example of a domain where past events more inevitably, regularly, and evidently (if not uniquely) *determine* the present resulting state. No phonologist today would reconstruct a proto-language's sound system without attention *both* to recognized universals of synchronic sound-systems *and* to attested (and phonetically motivated) paths of phonological change; it is assumed that the same perceptual, muscular, acoustic, and cognitive constraints are responsible for both universals of structure and universals of structural change. And, for a historical phonologist or semanticist trying to avoid imposing past analyses on present usage, it is an empirical question *which* aspects of diachrony are preserved in a given synchronic phonological structure or meaning structure.

A third area showing regularities parallel to those observed in polysemy and semantic change is pragmatic ambiguity. A word or phrase is called ambiguous when it has two different meanings, or semantic values. But it is also possible for a linguistic form to have only one semantic value, but multiple functions nonetheless. A salient example is the pragmatic ambiguity of negation (Horn 1985). Horn argues that *not* really means the same thing in "She's not happy, she's sad" and "She's not happy, she's ecstatic." The difference is that in the first case the negative semantics is understood as being applied to the *content* of the word *happy*, while in the second case it is applied to some understood assertability (or some other pragmatic aspect)[11] of the first clause. (We understand the second example above as meaning something like "I would not *say* she was happy, but rather I would *say* she was ecstatic.") That is to say, the use rather than the sense of the negation is what varies.

In order to explain this particular example, we need to understand what assertability is (what does it mean to say that assertability can be negated, as opposed to content?). If we had a purely truth-conditional theory of semantics, it is hard to see how we could explain usages like "She's not happy, she's ecstatic," wherein an utterance including the (apparently not contradicted) words "She's not happy" *entails* the truth of "She's happy." But if our theory of meaning is centered around the speaker's cognitive system, then we might expect the speaker to have and express some structured understanding of the linguistic interchange itself. More than that, we might expect that in uttering a linguistic form, the speaker's idea of the current linguistic act would be a deeply seated background to the production and use of the form. And indeed it seems that the idea of asserting as a speech act is so basic to our cognitive systems that we don't even need to overtly talk about asserting in order to negate it. Notice that we *do* have to overtly mention a concept such as *happy* to negate its content. Only as part of an exchange concerning my happiness can a phrase like *No* or *I'm not* mean "I'm not happy". But *She's not happy, she's ecstatic* can mean "I wouldn't *call* her happy, I'd *call* her ecstatic" without anybody previously mentioning talking or calling – the fact that they're *doing* these things is enough background to ensure that we can evoke these speech acts as the understood subject-matter of a negation.

I am going to argue that our understanding of language use, and our understanding of cognition itself, are inherent underpinnings to all our use of language. We understand both these domains at least partly in terms of the external physical (and social) domain. And we use the same vocabulary in many cases to express relationships in the speech act and epistemic (reasoning) worlds that we use to express parallel relationships in the content domain (the "real-world" events and entities, sometimes including speech and thought, which form the content of speech and thought). Negation is an example.

Most past work on pragmatically conditioned meanings has in fact relied strongly on the structure of the speech-act world. It has been argued that expression of certain primary content, plus a knowledge of the context and the interlocutors' reasoning processes, allows indirect expression of some other content, which is *systematically* related to the first.[12] (For example, "It's cold in here," given some expectation that the addressee cares about the speaker's comfort, could convey "Please close the window.") What has not so far been argued is that any of the same cognitive structuring underlies both polysemy and pragmatic ambiguity. And that is what I propose to argue in chapters 3, 4, and 5.

In this book, I shall argue that a successful account of a large class of synchronic polysemy relations and pragmatic ambiguity cases can be given in the same framework independently needed to account for certain major trends in semantic change. But this unified analysis of synchronic and diachronic meaning-relations necessarily calls into question many of the commonest assumptions underlying current theoretical work in semantics.

The preceding discussion has tacitly raised a question to which I will not give a full answer right here, because I propose to spend most of the rest of the book answering it: why is a cognitively based approach the right way to tackle the issues of multiple form-to-function mappings? Before I can try to answer this, I need to give some overview of current understanding of semantic structure, and of the ways it has linked up with work on diachrony, polysemy, and pragmatics. This would be an immense task if undertaken in any complete sense, so I shall limit myself to the positions and works most directly relevant to my project.

Recent work in linguistics has tended to view semantics in one of two divergent ways: either meaning is a potentially mathematizable or formalizable domain (if only we could find the right primes or premises for the mathematical analysis), or meaning is a morass of culturally and historically idiosyncratic facts from which one can salvage occasional linguistic regularities. Those who do the former kind of semantics have frequently been eager to separate linguistic meaning from general human cognition and experience, and to keep linguistic "levels" (syntax vs semantics vs pragmatics) distinct from one another; formalization is presumed to be easier if the domain can be successfully delimited. Semanticists of the latter sort, on the other hand, are often quite ready to accept the direct influence of experience or cognition on meaning-structures, but find it hard to see how such meaning-structures could be formalized: how can airtight generalizations be made about experience-shaped semantics, when experience itself is so varied and so far from currently being described by any complete formal analysis?

I agree strongly with those semanticists who consider meaning to be rooted in human cognitive experience: experience of the cultural, social, mental, and physical worlds. But cognition is structured, not chaotic – and the apparently disorderly domain of linguistic meaning can often be shown to be structured around speakers' understanding of a given cognitive domain. Cognitive and experiential semantic analysis need not in principle be less formalizable than traditional objectivist feature-analyses of meaning. I shall argue, in fact, that formal feature-analyses of lexical items have missed crucial generalizations which can readily be expressed within a cognitively framed theory of meaning.

Systematic metaphorical connections link our vocabulary of the sociophysical domain with the epistemic and speech-act domains. Thus, for example, it is not by chance that *must* is polysemous between social obligation and logical certainty, although it would be hard to find a common objective feature of these meanings. Rather this polysemy relationship is part of a larger pattern discussed in chapter 3. These inter-domain connections are cognitively based, and they pervasively influence patterns of polysemy, semantic change, and sentence interpretation. Since such metaphorical connections are not based on objective similarities, my understanding of meaning cannot be an objectivist one. But neither is it subjectivist: rather, I assume that the real world exists, but our only access to it is through our experience, both physical and cultural. In a sense, this experientialist viewpoint (see G. Lakoff 1986) is less subjective than an objectivist viewpoint, since it seeks to explain the actual categories of human language and cognition, rather than presupposing that extant linguistic categories must have an objective basis (and therefore assuming that the objective "real world" must necessarily be structured like language). In order to give my approach an appropriate context, it is necessary first to discuss some of the prominent schools of semantic analysis and explain my differences with them; I shall then return to cognitive approaches to polysemy and semantic change.

1.1 Past approaches and problems

One common approach to lexical meaning has been to define each word as a bundle of formal semantic features (see Katz and Fodor 1963). So far as I know, no analyst has ever plausibly attempted to give a full feature analysis of even one word. The usual procedure has been to discuss the features relevant to the semantic or syntactic distinctions at hand (see Jackendoff 1972, for example). Individual word meaning was considered to be determined only relative to some contrast set, and to be interesting only insofar as it was reflected in concrete linguistic (particularly syntactic) behavior. In some ways this reflected an older structuralist viewpoint: Saussure (1959 [1915]) and his followers had been successful in making new generalizations about linguistic structure by assuming that structure, rather than content, was the crucial subject of analysis. American structuralism followed in this tradition; and generative grammar inherited from American structuralism the idea that word meaning was to be defined purely by semantic contrast-sets, just as Bloomfieldian phoneme-structure was to be defined purely by minimal pairs (rather than directly by phonetics).

Semantic analyses within the Katz–Fodor tradition have tried to account for a wide range of potential meaning-contrasts; they have been interested in entailment relations, contradiction, presupposition, and sentential synonymy, as well as simple lexical synonymy and contrast. But the focus has continued to be on those aspects of meaning which are relevant to differences between lexemes, not on a full account of meaning *per se*. (I am not, incidentally, intending to suggest that everything relevant to the meaning of a lexical item should necessarily be considered as *part* of the meaning. Although I take a richer view of lexical meaning than do many formal semanticists, such a view is perfectly compatible with a distinction (see Fillmore 1976; Searle 1983) between word meaning and the *frame* or *background* relative to which word meaning exists. I have argued [Sweetser 1986] in favor of such a distinction in the case of the verb *lie*.)

The most complete attempts at feature analyses have generally been studies of particular contrast sets within the vocabulary of some particular language (e.g. Lounsbury 1964). Lexical fields such as kinship terms or personal pronouns seem in fact to be naturally structured around a few basic and separable dimensions of contrast. These dimensions provide a naturally chosen group of relevant semantic parameters, used in most possible permutations – thus feature analysis initially seemed quite reasonable when applied to such domains. (This is not to say that any given feature analysis is correct, but simply that such domains share a self-contained and decomposable quality which makes them more amenable to feature analysis than many other areas of meaning.) But when applied to lexical semantics at large, feature semantics showed obvious limitations (see Bolinger 1965). One of its greatest difficulties was its underlying assumption of the existence of a limited number of semantic primes. This set of primes was a supposedly universal building-block set, a pre-fabricated kit, which came as part of each human's language-acquisition device. Different cultures might use these blocks to build different complex larger structures; but at some crucial level languages were assumed to share the basic units of meaning, just as basic syntactic categories such as N and V were considered to be universal. However, the task of actually cataloguing the primes for even one language has never been accomplished (nor credibly attempted),[13] and the general working attitude has been that the analyst just keeps on adding as many dimensions of meaning as are necessary to make sure that usage distinctions are accounted for. An "elegant" feature system postulates no more meaning dimensions than are necessary – i.e., such an analysis shrinks from proposing three or four semantic differences between two lexical items when one difference is all that is formally required to keep the words distinct from each other. (Again, meaning itself is not the central issue; meaning-contrasts are all that matter.) But no other limits besides "elegance" have been proposed to prevent proliferation of primes. Recent computational models have shown the same tendency: Schank and Abelson (1977) is a salient example of basically *ad hoc* creation of primes. Given this situation, claims of the universality of semantic primes are essentially vacuous.

Prominent

In the European tradition, semantic-field theorists such as Trier and Weisgerber looked at meanings as something more organic than feature bundles, and as being interrelated with many different aspects of human experience. The success of such an approach is due to its attention to relatively compact areas of vocabulary, where contrasts emerge more clearly than in an entire lexicon taken as a whole (see reviews by Basilius 1952; Öhman 1953). Attempts such as that of Osgood (Osgood, Suci, and Tannenbaum 1957; Osgood, May, and Miron 1975) to find meaning-dimensions relevant to a whole lexicon have, predictably, isolated extremely abstract parameters such as the *good–bad* dimension; and, even then, the results often seem to depend crucially on highly unnatural judgments by speakers. Field theory, on the other hand, is interested above all in the closely woven interrelationships within clearly delineated areas of meaning. Its limitation, of course, is that it does not immediately apply to the explanation of semantic relationships *between* fields. Thus field theory would find it as hard as componential-feature theory to explain why the vocabulary of vision should be regularly applied to the domain of knowledge.

Many theories on the small scale but become too abstract when dealing with an entire lexicon

Returning to the American tradition, it must be said that recent logically based (especially Montagovian) semantic work has largely ignored lexical semantics, preferring to assume that the predicates involved in semantic logical structures could somehow be defined, and to concentrate on the compositional regularities of combining lexical units. What lexical analysis has been done in this tradition (see Dowty 1979) has (as mentioned above) tended to be on the aspects of lexical meaning most relevant to compositionality. Syntactic and pragmatic analyses which crucially depend on such a semantic framework (e.g. Gazdar 1979; Gazdar *et al.* 1985) do so in the knowledge that their work will stand or

autonomy of words

fall to the extent that it proves actually possible to do a full lexical-semantic analysis of the kind they presuppose. Their assumption of autonomous levels, and of a purely compositional semantics, seems to me dubious in the light of recent research (see section 1.2). Although practitioners of such theories have sometimes claimed to be modelling human cognitive abilities, this claim is not very serious, given the isolation of Montague semantics from cultural, acquisitional, and other cognitive data.

The work presented in this book has both less and more ambitious goals than feature-oriented or logical formal-semantic analysis. Less ambitious, in that I tend to believe that a full account of lexical meaning will only come hand-in-hand with a far fuller understanding of cognition than is presently available, so my goals do not extend to a full catalogue of even the relevant aspects of meaning. More ambitious, in that I intend to describe and motivate generalizations which cannot be described in terms of objective features or logical truth-values.

1.2   Cognitively oriented recent work in semantics

In the last two decades, many researchers have begun arguing for a systematic analysis of language as rooted in general human cognitive abilities. Berlin and Kay's (1969) work on color terms, followed by Kay and MacDaniel's (1978) lexical-semantic analysis of basic color-terms, have proposed that human physiology underlies certain universal trends in semantics. Rosch's work (1973, 1978, and elsewhere) on basic-level categories, and Eve Clark's work (1976) comparing classifier systems with children's early acquisition of word meanings, have suggested that perceptual and interactional patterns are deeply involved in determination of lexical categories (see G. Lakoff's [1986] further analysis of linguistic categorization). Both Rosch and Clark throw serious doubt on an analysis of linguistic categories based on Boolean set-membership. Human categorization seems to form internally coherent classes, but the complements of these classes have no natural coherence or shared features – they are not treated as sets. Fillmore (1976, 1977, and elsewhere) and Coleman and Kay (1981) have argued for changes in our understanding of the internal structure of word meaning; in particular, the internal structure of word meaning is not autonomous but exists against a background of our general assumptions about the world (sociocultural beliefs included), and word meaning is frequently prototype-based rather than being composed of checklists of features. The prototypical use of a word will generally fit some normal, frequently encountered case; when deviation from that case occurs, then (a) the category boundaries are fuzzy, not like Boolean sets (G. Lakoff 1972), and (b) word meanings may not apply at all outside the relevant background assumptions (Sweetser 1986). In this approach, word meaning cannot be fully analyzed into features, since the meaning and its frame are inseparable from one another. The frame may not be part of the lexical meaning itself, but our understanding of meaning crucially involves analysis of both the frames and the lexical senses which depend on them.

Lakoff and Johnson (1980) have further proposed that linguistic usages frequently reflect our inherently metaphorical understanding of many basic areas of our lives; that is, not merely language but cognition (and *hence* language) operates metaphorically much of the time. Such claims (substantiated by a large corpus of data) would be very difficult to relate to a semantic analysis based solely on logical form and distinctive features. The kinds of "likeness" (e.g. cultural categorization of women, fire, and dangerous things into a class – see G. Lakoff 1987) and metaphors inherent in language do not seem to fall out neatly from the sort of (supposedly objective) features proposed by formal-lexical analysts. Rather, the metaphors manifested in most linguistic systems fall out from a more holistic viewpoint, which takes language as part of our general cognitive system: linguistic structure is, then, as logical and objective as human cognition, no more and no less.

At the level of sentence semantics, traditional formal analyses have also been questioned. It cannot be maintained that semantics is autonomous relative to syntax and pragmatics, nor that sentence semantics is purely compositional (see Fillmore, Kay, and O'Connor 1988). There seem to be not only lexical items (e.g., discourse particles) but syntactic structures whose purpose is to signal pragmatic goals. Gordon and Lakoff's (1971) study of structures such as "Why paint your house purple?" has shown that there are cases where a syntactic form (here, a *why*-question without *do you* following the *why*) is employed solely to mark a very specific pragmatic purpose (here, to suggest that the addressee should not do the action described). In general, it is also impossible to draw rigid boundaries between the logical and social aspects of meaning. Work on language acquisition has shown that even so-called logical concepts (such as causation or negation) are acquired through the child's social and physical experience (Bates, Camaioni, and Volterra 1979; Volterra and Antinucci

1979). Indeed, linguistic acquisition is impossible until general cognitive development is at the right stage for the acquisition of that area of meaning (Slobin 1973 and elsewhere).

I will base my analysis on this body of cognitively oriented linguistic research, and also on the general traditions of pragmatic analysis and speech-act theory, which will be discussed in more detail at the appropriate points in the ensuing chapters. Like cognitive-linguistic analyses, speech-act theory has succeeded in rooting our understanding of language use in our knowledge of broader human behavioral patterns.

Recent research in historical semantics has brought out regularities in semantic change and has highlighted the extent to which meaning-change, as well as meaning itself, is structured by cognition. Particularly interesting parallels can be drawn between the work on child language-acquisition (e.g. H. Clark 1973) and work on the historical development of spatial terms (e.g. Traugott 1982 and elsewhere): both show temporal vocabulary following and emerging from spatial vocabulary. Givón (1973) and Fleischman (1982a, 1982b, 1983) demonstrate a similar relationship between spatial motion verbs and tense markers. In general (see Traugott 1982) it seems clear that more abstract domains of meaning tend to derive their vocabulary from more concrete domains (rather than vice versa) and, furthermore, that in some cases there is a deep cognitive predisposition to draw from certain particular concrete domains in deriving vocabulary for a given abstract domain. What we would like to know is more about the connections between concrete and abstract domains (what makes space a good source for time vocabulary, for example?). And this brings us precisely to the question of what is *related* to what in our meaning-structures: the central question for any examination of what motivates form–function mappings. Which, in turn, brings us to metaphor, as one crucial, but often ignored, source of links between multiple senses of a single form.

1.3   Semantic change and polysemy patterns: metaphorical connections between semantic fields

As was mentioned above, local studies of the systemic contrasts which structure particular semantic fields often reveal fascinating aspects of our linguistic and cognitive treatment of these areas of meaning, and may well tell us much about what meanings within the domain are "close" to each other, and what meanings are likely to be historically connected. But such studies leave unaddressed the mass of metaphorically structured polysemy data, and the fact that metaphor is a major structuring force in semantic change. Metaphor operates *between* domains. It operates so pervasively that speakers find an inter-domain connection between knowledge and vision, or between time and space, to be as natural as the intra-domain connections between *finger* and *hand* or between *man* and *woman*. Studies of systematic metaphorical connections between domains are thus needed, in addition to local studies of relevant semantic contrasts, to help us understand what is a likely relationship between two senses.

Why insist on talking about metaphor, rather than just some general idea of connections between domains: why is it insufficient to say that, for example, knowledge and vision are connected? The knowledge/vision case will be discussed in detail in the following chapter, but let us briefly examine another parallel case. Traugott and Dasher (1985) and Traugott (in press) have shown that physical-domain verbs frequently come to have speech-act and/or mental-state meanings, and mental-state verbs come to have speech-act meanings, while the opposite directions of change do not occur. First, the unidirectionality of these shifts might be explained by the inherent unidirectionality of a metaphorical connection (viewing X as Y is not the same as, and does not imply, viewing Y as X). Further, I have argued (Sweetser 1987b) that two overlapping but distinct systems of metaphors connect the vocabulary of physical action/motion/location with the domains of mental states and speech acts. Both speech acts and mental states are metaphorically treated as travel through space. Note, as an English example, the parallelism between the *about/over* contrast in the physical domain – *go over the house* indicates more thorough physical coverage than *go around/about the house* – and in the mental-state and speech-act domains: *think about* vs *think over, talk about* vs *talk over* (something which I have "thought over" has been given more thorough mental coverage than if I had just "thought about" it). Further examples of the lively metaphorical treatment of speech and thought as travel include examples (1)–(4):

(1) How *far had we gotten* when we were interrupted?
(2) Let's *go over* that discussion again.
(3) I think I'm *getting somewhere* with that problem.
(4) What conclusion have you *come to/reached*?

To this extent, the domains of reasoning and speech exchange are metaphorically structured in terms of the same physical activities.

However, a journey is not our only metaphorical structuring of these two domains, and the other metaphorical structurings appear to be particular to one domain or the other. Speech acts are metaphorically treated as exchange or transfer of objects from one interlocutor to the other; the objects are linguistic forms, which are containers for meaning. This object-exchange metaphor for speech exchange has been analyzed under the name of "the conduit metaphor" (see Reddy 1979). The conduit metaphor is evidenced in such metaphorical phrases as *empty words* (which have no *content*); *get your meaning across to the reader*; *what did you get out of that talk*; *take/accept an offer/an apology*; and also in etymologies like *pro-pose* < "put forward" or *re-fuse* < "pour back". Speech exchange, and argument in particular, is also metaphorically understood as combat: you can "stand your ground" when your interlocutor "attacks your position," and parallel etymologies like *in-sist* (< "stand on, stand one's ground") give evidence of the same metaphor. Metaphors for mental states, on the other hand, do not typically include either combat or object exchange (presumably because reasoning is viewed as a largely individual activity, rather than a two-participant one). There is, however, strong evidence that mental activity is seen as *manipulation* and *holding* of objects: we "grasp" a new idea; "discard" a faulty assumption; or use a hypothesis as "building-block" in the "foundations" of a theory. Etymologically, parallel semantic developments are to be observed in *hypothesize* (< "put under," as a foundation), *comprehend* (< "grasp"), or *surmise* (< "put on/over," i.e. on top of what is already hypothesized).[14]

My claim, then, is that only by examining the particular metaphorical mappings involved in our cognitive and linguistic treatment of mental states and speech acts can we make sense of the fact that certain physical-state and motion verbs are likely sources for vocabulary of certain abstract areas of meaning, while other physical-state/motion verbs systematically come to have different abstract meanings. In general, it is true that speech and intellectual activity are metaphorically referred to in terms from the domain of physical action, but there are also significant generalizations to be observed at a lower level. It is not by chance that the etymological sources of speech-act and mental-state verbs overlap in certain areas and are distinct in others.

The chapters which follow comprise a set of studies of four distinct semantic areas: perception verbs; modality; conjunction; and *if–then* conditionals. I shall argue that the semantics of all four of these lexical fields are inherently structured by our multi-leveled cultural understanding of language and thought. In particular, we model our understanding of logic and thought processes on our understanding of the social and physical world; and simultaneously, we model linguistic expression itself not only (a) as description (a model of the world), but also (b) as action (an act in the world being described), and even (c) as an epistemic or logical entity (a premise or a conclusion in our world of reasoning). Not only do the semantics of these lexical fields, taken collectively, constitute a strong argument for metaphorically structured cognitive and linguistic understanding of the relevant areas, but they may also throw some light on the interaction between semantics/pragmatics and syntactic structure.

Cognitive-semantic studies of polysemy structures (Lindner 1981; Brugman 1983, 1984, 1988) have succeeded in uncovering motivation and order behind previously random-looking groupings of meanings. Using the idea of systematic metaphorical structuring of one domain (e.g. the epistemic domain) in terms of another (e.g. the sociophysical domain), cognitive semantics may well be equipped to make headway in the murky area of meaning-change, as well as in the area of synchronic semantic structure.

Chapter 2 is a historical case-study of English and Indo-European sense-perception verbs. Deep and pervasive metaphorical connections link our vocabulary of physical perception and our vocabulary of intellect and knowledge. An objective, Boolean-feature-based semantic theory could not explain such a connection, but a cognitively based theory accounts for it readily and naturally. Further, as in the conduit-metaphor case discussed above, a metaphorical analysis motivates the otherwise strange fact that certain semantic sub-domains within perception are naturally and regularly historical sources for certain sub-domains of cognition, rather than for others.

Chapter 3 examines English modal verbs in the light of the metaphorical structures discussed in the preceding chapter. It is possible to give a unified analysis of the contrast between root and epistemic modality, and of some further uses of modal verbs which cannot properly be described as either root or epistemic, by appealing to the notion of metaphorical structuring of the domains of cognition and of speech exchange in terms of the more external domains of physical and social interaction. An appeal to such a metaphorical structuring of these domains is supported (for the epistemic domain) by the evidence laid out in chapter 2, and (for both domains) by historical-semantic work such as Traugott (in press), Traugott and Dasher

(1985), and Sweetser (1987b). Similarities between the behavior of root and epistemic modals, and also some apparently idiosyncratic differences between the two, can be shown to fall out naturally from an appropriate understanding of the different natures of the domains in which they operate, and hence from our understanding of these domains as metaphorically identified with each other.

Chapters 4 and 5 extend the analysis further, arguing that sentence conjunction and *if–then* conditionals must also be understood against a background of this network of inter-domain metaphorical connections. Conjunction and conditionality, I claim, are subject to interpretation in the epistemic and speech-act domains, as well as in the sociophysical domain. Thus it is not simply the interpretation or the history of individual lexical items which is shaped by this cognitive structure. Our interpretation of sentence semantics, and in particular of the relationships between clauses, is influenced as well, including traditionally "logical" relationships such as *and*, *or*, and *if*. Although logical operators have been assumed to be the simplest part of language for objective logical analysis, in fact their use cannot be successfully described without reference to experientially based cognitive structure.

I shall not be arguing that conjunctions such as *and* have multiple semantic values, but rather that they have meanings so general that they apply equally to our conceptions of the sociophysical, epistemic, and speech-act domains. But this is only true given certain metaphorical understandings of the epistemic and speech-act domains – for example, the understanding of reasoning processes as following a *spatially linear trajectory sequentially moving from one point to another*.

It is of particular interest to notice that the same cognitive structure underlies (a) polysemy patterns in lexical meaning; (b) historical patterns in meaning-change; and (c) multiple possibilities for interpretation of conjoined or conditional sentences. In particular, there is persistent parallelism between formal markers of aspects of content, aspects of the speaker's reasoning, and aspects of the current speech-act. There is evidence that this metaphorical structure is not restricted to Indo-European; if it represents any universal semantic tendencies, then this work may be of further use to analysts beyond the limited linguistic area here described. In any case, formal feature-based semantic analysis would not be able to account for the observed regularities; while a cognitively based analysis can not only describe the observed meaning patterns naturally and elegantly, but motivate them and explain them.

2   *Semantic structure and semantic change: English perception-verbs in an Indo-European context*[1]

2.1   Introduction

As mentioned in chapter 1, recent work on polysemy structures (see Brugman 1988; G. Lakoff 1985) has suggested that a word meaning is a structured and unified entity. In order to better understand that structure, we need further investigation of the connections between the different (sub-)meanings of polysemous lexical items. In phonology, analysts have frequently assumed that units which were related, or could be classed together, would be more likely to undergo parallel historical changes. For the restricted semantic field of English perception-verbs, this chapter will investigate the interaction between synchronic semantic groupings and parallelisms in historical change of meaning. I shall argue that the historical and synchronic data point to one and the same cognitively based analysis of the relevant semantic domain.

The general study of semantic change has undergone a long period of relative neglect, largely because the phonological part of word history proved so much more immediately tractable to systematic analysis. Semantic shifts have been felt to be random, whimsical, and irregular; general rules concerning them are nearly impossible to establish.[2] Of course, two hundred years ago the same charges might well have been leveled against phonological change, and only work based on the opposite assumption of regularity could have changed our understanding of sound change as it has been changed since then. But it is scarcely surprising that to many linguists, the non-phonological side of etymology appears inherently non-scientific. Synchronic as well as diachronic linguistics has found sound a more accessible domain for study than meaning. There are natural limits set by our vocal and auditory physiology to the possible

23

(1a)

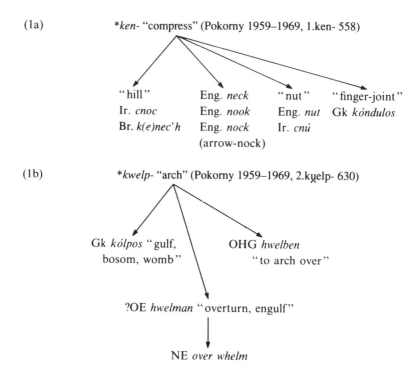

ken- "compress" (Pokorny 1959–1969, 1.ken- 558)

"hill"   Eng. *neck*   "nut"   "finger-joint"
Ir. *cnoc*   Eng. *nook*   Eng. *nut*   Gk *kóndulos*
Br. *k(e)nec'h* Eng. *nock*   Ir. *cnú*
                (arrow-nock)

(1b)

kwelp- "arch" (Pokorny 1959–1969, 2.kⱕelp- 630)

Gk *kólpos* "gulf,   OHG *hwelben*
   bosom, womb"   "to arch over"

?OE *hwelman* "overturn, engulf"

NE *over whelm*

parameters involved in phonology. Semantics is limited only by our capacity for meaning, i.e. by our cognitive capacity, which is dauntingly ill-understood in comparison to the physical limits of the vocal tract. And yet lexical semantics, and semantic change, have frequently been analyzed as based on groupings of features, the semantic analogues of phonological distinctive features. Semantic feature-analyses, and feature-based etymologies such as those in (1a) and (1b), abound in the literature. In these etymologies, the supposed common semantic *feature* of the descendent words is the *compressed state* or *arched shape*; this feature is viewed as being retained by the descendent lexemes, while other features are added or dropped. The parallel to phonological rules is again evident; change is equivalent to feature addition or feature loss. The resulting proto-meaning thus becomes a sort of "lowest common denominator" of the descendent meanings.

If we took these feature-based semantic etymologies in general at their face value, the resulting Proto-Indo-European vocabulary as a whole would be an improbably abstract one.[3] It is widely acknowledged that basic vocabulary terms are the most likely to survive in a number of descendent languages, and hence to be securely reconstructible. Thanks to studies by Rosch (1977, 1978) and Mervis and Rosch (1981), we have some idea of a plausible abstractness-level for basic vocabulary items; and that level is much closer to the level of abstractness represented by Eng. *neck* or Gk *kólpos* than to the level of the proposed ancestral semantics of **kwelp-* or **ken-*. Furthermore, such generalizations about semantic change as we do have (see Stern 1931; Benveniste 1969, 1971; Traugott 1974, 1982; Fleischman 1982) suggest very strongly that meaning more frequently shifts from concrete to abstract than in the opposite direction; an observation which makes the semantic side of many feature-based etymologies doubly suspect.

This is not to say that there are not relevant parameters of semantic contrast, with respect to which words may change their meanings; but such parameters are more complex and less objective than feature analysts have thought them. As discussed in the preceding chapter, much of meaning is grounded in speakers' understanding of the world; and in particular, metaphorical semantic relationships cannot readily be described as simply changing a single feature or even a group of features – what must instead be described is a mapping of one domain onto another. Further, even in describing simpler changes which look more like traditional feature addition or feature loss, analysts should be aware that it is easier to retrace the history of added semantic features (eliminating them from the proto-semantics) than to reconstruct lost parameters. And when a parameter is only relevant to the semantics of one single descendent language, that does not necessarily mean it was a late addition to the semantics of the word. Only a general theory of naturalness in semantic change will tell us which descendent-language senses of a proto-morpheme are likely to be conservative ones.

As mentioned in chapter 1, European semantic-field analyses have sometimes shown more attention to grounding meaning in the relevant physical and social domains than has American feature-based semantics. They have thus often been successful in realistically assessing the relevant parameters of meaning within a domain. But semantic-field analyses cannot explain why polysemy and semantic change frequently cross between fields – for example, why (as will be discussed in this chapter) *see* and *know* should be related concepts. Semantic polysemy relationships, and semantic changes, frequently involve such metaphorical mappings, which cannot be described as simple features or parameters at all. When a semantic change such as "white" coming to mean "candid" occurs, any perceived sharing of parameters between whiteness and honesty is completely dependent on a broader understanding of moral qualities in terms of colors – an understanding which is neither objective nor readily expressible in terms of features.

What I am arguing is not, or not *yet*, that any specific proposed etymologies or reconstructed proto-senses of morphemes are wrong. My point is that the semantic side of the whole corpus of received etymological research is subject to question, because we have little or no idea of what constitutes a reasonable semantic reconstruction, and are only starting to be aware of what regularities may be generally observable in semantic change. There has been some excellent work in historical semantics, often by researchers whose thorough knowledge of the older Indo-European languages and good "feel" for word usage have enabled them to establish intuitively satisfying etymologies in cases where the descendent words would never have had a common denominator of feature. Since work on the older Indo-European languages inevitably entails work on poetic texts, there has also been fascinating elucidation of the shared and potentially reconstructible features of Indo-European poetic language, and even specific metaphors and formulae.[4] This work may, in my view, be more helpful to the reconstruction of a realistic Indo-European lexical semantics than comparison of isolated lexical meanings. But early research in Indo-European philology often paid little attention to realism in the proto-semantics, since the researchers in question were focusing on the detailed mapping of phonological and morphological relationships within the Indo-European language family. Without such work historical semantics would naturally be an impossible endeavor. But realism in semantic reconstruction has recently taken on increasing importance, as researchers (following Benveniste's brilliant lead) have attempted to use reconstructed word-meanings as a data-base for investigating the Indo-European proto-culture and its history. Given such use of proto-semantics, there is a sudden need for a realistic model of meaning-change; if we are arguing from reconstructed Indo-European phytonyms to some hypothesis about the location of the Indo-European homeland, it behooves us to know whether the meaning "tree" or "oak" or "strong, trustworthy" is the historically prior sense of the root *deru-* (see Friedrich 1979). We cannot assume that a proto-semantics based largely on the formal simplicity of supposed feature-changes (that is, a proto-semantics which is essentially a mnemonic for the groupings of the various descendent meanings) will necessarily also be a likely semantics for a real language spoken by a real community, nor that it will be a likely source for the proposed changes.

Recent work in historical semantics has been particularly lively in the area of grammaticalization – linguists such as Fleischman (1982a, 1982b, 1983), Mithun (1980), and others have studied the routes by which words travel from lexical-content word status to grammatical morpheme status. Perhaps even more interestingly, Traugott (1974, 1982) has mapped the historical semantic development of whole classes of English words from the propositional domain (morphemes that constitute the content of what is said) to the textual domain (morphemes whose meanings set out the structure of the discourse), and thence to the expressive domain (morphemes whose meanings are the speaker's affective commentary on the content of the discourse).[5] Traugott's more recent work (1986, 1987, 1988, 1989) has reformulated the earlier framework in terms of development from less to more *situated* in the speaker's mental attitude. (For example, use of demonstratives may involve identifying objects in the actual physical setting; but when a demonstrative becomes a definite article, it takes on the function of marking an entity as presumed to be mentally accessible for the purposes of the speech interaction, regardless of physical presence.) Evolutionary directions in word history from lexical to grammatical and from less to more situated seem well established at this point, and often correlate well with earlier observations of the prevalence of change from concrete to abstract. Very recently, Traugott has given particularly interesting explanations of semantic change in terms of metonymic and pragmatic restructuring of meaning.[6] Bybee (1985) also examines the semantic developments (including abstraction) which accompany morphologization. Such research has laid the groundwork in crucial areas of historical semantics.

But in a more general way, what connects one meaning with another, and how does semantic change occur? Even given a concrete-to-abstract direction, how does one element in the concrete domain become associated with a specific abstract meaning, rather than with some other meaning? Or how do meanings shift within a domain? This chapter is an attempt to map out the systematic connections between meanings – the routes of semantic change – for the domain of English perception-verbs. The mappings I will be examining are examples of the sort of metaphorically structured, non-objective connections between senses which I have discussed above. My purpose is to increase our general understanding of both semantic relatedness and semantic change.[7]

2.2   The Mind-as-Body Metaphor

I will begin by offering several historical puzzles, all of which I intend to resolve in the course of this chapter.

1. Why should words for physical likeness come to mean probability? There is a plethora of examples. Eng. *like* and *likely* are of course instances of the same etymon; MIr. *samlaid* "likely" (cognate with Lat. *similitudo*) gives Mod.Ir. *amlaid* "likely";[8] Wel. *tebyg* means both "like" and "likely."

2. Why should "hear" come to mean "obey"? This I shall discuss in detail; the case I have primarily in mind is IE **k'leu-s-*, which gives Gk *klúo:* "hear," Eng. *listen*, Dan. *lystre* "obey," and Rus. *slušat'* "listen to"/*slušat's'a* "obey."

3. What connects physical holding (or manipulation) with intellectual understanding? This link is absolutely pervasive. Lat. *comprehendere* "seize" is the ancestor of Fr. *comprendre* "understand"; Gk *katalambáno:* "seize" (used metaphorically also to mean "understand") became Mod. Gk *katalambaíno:* "understand"; cf. Eng. "*grasp* a concept", or "*catch onto* an idea", or Fr. *j'ai saisi* "I have seized", which carried precisely the ambiguity of Eng. *gotcha*.

4. Why should words meaning "path" come to mean "however"? This too is a common shift exemplified by English *anyway* and by It. *tuttavia* ("anyway," lit. "all road"), and possibly by cases such as Br. *forzh* "however, no matter," if the latter is cognate with Wel. *fordd* "path" and Eng. *ford*.

In order to solve these puzzles, I must first examine in some detail a semantic linkup which I shall call the "Mind-as-Body Metaphor." Kurath (1921) notes that Indo-European words for the emotions are very frequently derived from words referring to physical actions or sensations accompanying the relevant emotions, or to the bodily organs affected by those physical reactions. (For example, the heart's physical function of blood-pumping is strongly and noticeably affected by love, excitement, fear, and other strong emotions; therefore the heart comes to symbolize some of those strong emotions – such as courage or passion. Or, because physical brightness is conducive to cheerfulness, "bright" comes to mean cheerful, while "dull" means the reverse.) This trend conforms to the previously mentioned generalization that change proceeds from concrete to abstract. Kurath is inclined to attribute this historical development of emotion words to the psychosomatic nature of the emotions: that is, to the inseparability of physical sensation from emotional reaction, or of emotional state from concomitant physical changes. He may well be right in assuming that such a link is at the root of our tendency to derive our vocabulary of the mind from our vocabulary of the body; but it is hard to see how such a link-up could be very directly present in many of the cases. Thus for example, psychological tests have shown that physical colors (e.g., of the walls of a room) do affect people's emotional state; it would seem that bright colors do indeed help promote "bright" moods. Likewise, emotional *tension* or feeling *low* can be linked to physical muscular states of tension or limpness which accompany the relevant mental states. But uses such as *bitter* anger and *sweet* personality seem relatively distinct from any direct physical taste-response of sweetness or bitterness. I would regard such uses of *bitter* and *sweet* as metaphorical: the anger is unpleasant to our emotions in a way analogous to that in which a bitter taste displeases our tastebuds.

Even in cases such as *bright*, where there is apparently some actual correlation between physical world and emotional state, there is not, of course, a necessary correlation. That is to say, it is perfectly possible to be depressed in a well-lit room with yellow walls. Here I would like to introduce an important theoretical distinction, namely that between a partial but commonplace correlation in experience and a full metaphorical mapping. Lakoff and Johnson (1980) examine the metaphor "More is Up." They note that *often*, in what are perhaps prototypical physical cases, there is an actual correlation between our perception of increasing quantity and our perception of upwards motion: for example, the surface of a liquid rises as more liquid is poured into the container, or a pile of objects gets higher as more objects are added to it. But, of course, in other cases (as in liquid poured out on a flat surface and allowed to spread laterally – or as in less concrete cases, where the very idea of quantity may be metaphorical: "more knowledge" or "more love") there may be no such correlation. But the existing correlation in the prototypical cases has *motivated* a more general metaphorical mapping, so that "More" is mapped onto "Up" whether or not there is any correlation observed. Thus we can say "The number of cat hairs on my black dress has *risen* since I got a white cat."

My point is that the Mind-as-Body Metaphor is very probably *motivated* by correlations between our external experience and our internal emotional and cognitive states, but the correlations alone will not explain the observed patterns of polysemy and semantic change. In order to explain the fact that the mappings are much fuller than the correlations, we need another, more general kind of connection between the two domains. We would also like to explain the fact that the mappings are [unidirectional:] bodily experience is a source of vocabulary for our psychological states, but not the other way around. The correlations are bidirectional and partial, but the mapping observed in semantic change and in synchronic metaphorical language is both unidirectional and more general than the correlations. Its unidirectionality alone would suggest the possibility that it is metaphorical in nature.

Further examples of this metaphorical extension of our physical vocabulary are numerous, and many of them are totally inexplicable in psychosomatic terms. For example, in English (and in the Indo-European family at large) our lexicon of logic, causation, and conversational structure is based on our more concrete sociophysical lexicon. The *must* of "You *must* be home by ten, or I'll tell Mother" describes a real-world force or necessity imposed by the utterance. But the same word *must* refers likewise to logical necessity, as in "John *must* be home; I see his coat" (see Sweetser 1982). Further, the abstract logical (epistemic) meaning of the English modals is historically later than their more concrete sociophysical ("root" or "deontic") usage (see Shepherd 1981, 1982; Traugott 1982, 1988). *May* meant physical ability before it came to mean social permission or logical possibility.

I can see no objective semantic feature linking sociophysical force or ability with logical certainty or possibility; neither can I see any psychosomatic link between the two senses of the English modal verbs. The only possible link between the epistemic and deontic domains is metaphorical: we view logical necessity, for example, as being the mental analogue of sociophysical force, while logical possibility is the mental (or epistemic) analogue of permission or ability in the real world. The continuing liveliness of this metaphor (which certainly is no longer a *consciously* figurative usage in the case of the modal verbs) can easily be seen in current expressions such as "a *strong* argument," "a *weak* premise," "a *forced* conclusion," etc.

It is not only modal verbs which show this tendency to multi-domain usage: causal conjunctions, speech-act verbs, and other lexical fields show

multidomain
usage

widespread semantic developments of the same type (see Sweetser 1982). The causality in "He loves me *because* I remind him of his first love" is basic sociophysical causality; but "He loves me, *because* he wouldn't have proofread my whole thesis if he didn't" does not express the same kind of causation. A paraphrase "I *conclude* that he loves me *because* I *know* that he wouldn't otherwise have proofread my thesis" shows us what the real causal relations are in the sentence so paraphrased. The point is that we use precisely the same repertory of causal conjunctions to indicate causation of one event by another, and "causation" of a conclusion by a premise.

Conversational causation may also be expressed using the same forms which mark causation in the sociophysical and epistemic worlds: in "What are you doing tonight? – *because* there's a good movie on," the causation is not between the content of the second and first clauses, but rather between the content of the second clause and the performance of the speech act expressed by the first clause. The understanding of force and causality in the speech-act world in terms of sociophysical force is visible elsewhere in the language as well: "What was the *force* of that statement?" The linguistic and philosophical concept of speech-act *force* is highly coherent (to say the least) with folk ways of referring to the same set of phenomena; we speak of linguistic acts as having the kind of causal effects which non-linguistic acts have, presumably largely because we in fact use speech acts to achieve many of the social goals that we would otherwise have to achieve by action.

Traugott's (1982 and elsewhere) observations concerning the movement from propositional to textual to expressive meanings give clear evidence for the same kind of development in many other domains; her propositional level corresponds fairly closely to my sociophysical level, and her textual level coincides at least partially with my epistemic level. There is, then, a general tendency to borrow concepts and vocabulary from the more accessible physical and social world to refer to the less accessible worlds of reasoning, emotion, and conversational structure.

So we are left with the following conclusions: (a) the link-up between our vocabularies of mind and body may have some psychosomatic roots, but it is essentially metaphorical in nature, and this equation of the physical self and the inner self is pervasive in English and in the Indo-European family at large (if indeed it is not a universal); (b) we would profit from a clearer understanding of how one particular unit of meaning on the sociophysical level becomes connected with a particular semantic category at the abstract mental level, rather than with some other category. (Why does *ability* come to mean *possibility*, rather than *necessity*, for example? Or why does *heart* come to mean *courage* or *love*, rather than *fear*?) Given the general Mind-as-Body Metaphor as a background, in the following sections I will try to explicate the connections between the (earlier) concrete and (historically later) abstract meanings of perception verbs in English.

2.3   Sense-perception verbs in English and Indo-European

I shall now map out the historical routes into and out of the domain of physical perception in English, with a view to their detailed interpretation in the next section. What are the sources of English perception-verbs, and for what other domains is the perception lexicon itself a historical source?

2.3.1   Vision

1. The common semantic sources for vision verbs are:

   (a)   The physical nature of sight (light, the eyes, facial movement, etc.)

        Eng. *to eye* (from the noun *eye*)
        LGer. *oegen* (< *oog*) > Eng. *ogle*
        ghei- "yawn" > Eng. *gape, gawp*
        ster- "firm, stiff" > Eng. *stare*
        leuk- "light" > Eng. *light*, Lat. *lux*, Wel. *golug* "sight," and Gk *leuk-* "white."

   (b)   Metaphors of vision
        (i) *Vision ⇐ physical touching, manipulation.* This metaphor is discussed in Lakoff and Johnson (1980). Its probable basis is the channeling and focusing ability connected with our visual sense; vision, far more than the other senses, can pick out ("seize on") and attend to one stimulus amid a multitude of input stimuli. Examples:

           be*hold*, *catch* sight of
           per*ceive* (< Lat. *-cipio* "seize") (both general and visual meanings)
           scrutinize (< Lat. *scrutari* "pick through trash")
           examine (< Lat. *ex + agmen-* "pull out from a row")
           discern (< Lat. *dis-cerno* "separate")
           see (< *sek^w-*, which also gives Lat. *sequor* "follow")

        (ii) *Visual monitoring ⇔ control.* The basis for this metaphor is probably the fact that guarding or keeping control often involves visual monitoring of the controlled entity; and the limited domain of physical vision is further analogous to the domain of personal influence or control. Thus *weg-* "be strong, be lively" gives Eng. *watch* as well as *wake*, and (via French and Latin) *surveillance* as well as *vigil*. Likewise *scope*, which in English has come to refer to the sphere of control ("That problem is beyond my scope") is from the root of Gk *skópos*, meaning "sight, aim" in the physical sense.

(c) Basic Indo-European vision roots: There is a set of basic Indo-European roots which seem to have referred to vision as far back as their history can be traced. Examples are:

spek'- > Lat. *specere, -spicere* "look" > Eng. *inspect*
weid- > Lat. *videre*, Gk *eîdon* "see"; also Eng. *witness*
derk'- > Gk *dérkomai* "see, look," Wel. *edrych* "look"
(*ok^w-* "eye" – various verbs, possibly denominatives, such as Gk *ópsomai*, future of *horáo:* "see").
(s)wer- "watch, guard" – Gk *horáo:* "see," *éphoros* "guardian, overseer" (also possibly cognate with OE *waru*, NE *be-ware*; hence also with the Germanic-derived *guard* and *regard*, come into English from Old French).

2. Target domains for vision verbs. Vision verbs commonly develop abstract senses of mental activity:

(a) *Physical sight* ⇒ *knowledge, intellection*. This metaphor has its basis in vision's primary status as a source of data; not only does English have expressions like "I saw it with my own eyes" to indicate certainty, but studies of evidentials in many languages show that direct visual data is considered to be the most certain kind of knowledge.[9] Examples:

weid- "see":
Gk *eîdon* "see," perf. *oîda* "know" (> Eng. *idea*)
Eng. *wise, wit* (alongside the more physical *witness*)
Lat. *video* "see"
Ir. *fios* "knowledge"
(Note also that *sek^w-* is the ancestor of Hittite *sakk-/sekk-* "know," as well as of Eng. *see*)

(b) *Physical vision* ⇒ *mental "vision."* This metaphor is probably based on the strong connection between sight and knowledge, and also on the shared structural properties of the visual and intellectual domains – our ability to focus our mental and visual attentions, to monitor stimuli mentally and visually.

Ambiguous Germanic-derived cases which have either a physical or a mental sense are: *look down on, look up to, look forward to, look back on, overlook, look after.*

Cases which have now essentially only a mental meaning are: *oversee, hindsight, see to, foresee.*

In order to understand these examples, it is necessary to bring in other metaphors besides the understanding of mental "vision" as analogous to physical sight. Future is understood as forward, while past is backward (see Fillmore 1982); up is the direction of authority, while down symbolizes subjection (see Lakoff and Johnson 1980). Thus *hindsight* looks to the past, and *foresight* to the future; *overseeing* is done by an authority figure, and social inferiors may be *looked down on*. An example of the pervasiveness of this metaphor in the Indo-European family can be found in the case of the word *overseer*: English has borrowed the precisely parallel Latin and Greek compounds *supervisor* and *epi-skopos* (the adjective *episcopal* has retained its Greek root-form, although the noun *bishop* has been phonologically assimilated to English); all three of these compounds coexist in modern English usage.

From the Latin *spec-* and *vid-* roots, just as from the Germanic roots, we find that English has both physical and abstract descendents. Some words which have remained in the physical domain are *inspect, spectator, vista, view, survey, vision* (some of these have abstract uses as well). Cases which are purely in the mental domain are *suspect, respect, expect, retrospect, prospect, supervise, evident, provide, prudent (< pro-vid-ent-), envy (< in-vid-ia), revise, advise, interview, clairvoyance.* *Perceive, discern,* and *observe* all indicate intellectual as well as physical "vision," but in these cases it is possible that the original meanings (physical grasping, picking out, and being attentive to) may have come to mean mental attention or grasping at least as early as they came to mean vision. Our mental-focusing abilities are described by vocabulary drawn directly from the domain of physical manipulation, as well as by vocabulary from the domain of vision (see section 2.4).

2.3.2   Hearing

IE words for hearing often come from the physical domain. Thus, for example, Lat. *audire* goes back to an extension **aus-dh-* of the root **aus-* "ear". Various derivatives of the Indo-European root meaning "hear" or "listen," **k'leu-s-*, are preserved in descendents such as Gk *klúo :,* Mod.Ir. *cloisim,* Wel. *clywed* (all meaning "hear"), Eng. *listen,* and Rus. *slušat'* "listen."

The meanings derived from "hear" are, however, far more interesting than the semantic sources of hearing-verbs. Buck (1949) notes the surprising fact that nominals derived from Indo-European verbs of hearing generally do not denote sound (the physical thing heard); rather, they almost invariably denote the content of heard speech. Words for physical sound have most commonly an onomatopoetic origin – for example, Eng. *crash, bang*, or *pop; sound* and its relatives from the *son-* root in Latin; or Gk *e:ché:/é:cho:*. Words coming from *hear*-roots mean "tale, report, fame, glory, news." Thus, although Cl.Gk *klúo:* still retains the meaning "hear," its nominal and adjectival derivates, and the related verb *kléo:*, have all taken on this new meaning: *kléos* (*k'léwos*, ~ Skt *śrávas*) "fame, glory," *klutós* "famous," *kléo:* "celebrate, make famous." The Latin cognate *cluere* has the meaning "be famous." Similarly, Gk *akoúo:*, also meaning "hear," has the derived nominal *akoé:* (Homeric *akoué:*), meaning "hearing, thing heard, report."

Verbs of hearing themselves often come to mean "listen, heed" – thus, we have Eng. *listen* cognate with Gk *klúo:* from a root meaning "hear," as mentioned earlier. From "heed" we have a further semantic shift to "obey" – Dan. *lystre* "obey" also descends from the *k'leu-s*-root, and Russian has *slušat's'a* "obey" alongside *slušat'* "listen."

An interesting feature of the hear–heed semantic change is that the opposite direction also seems to be possible: words meaning mental attention or understanding can come to mean physical hearing. Thus, Lat. *intendere* "stretch out, direct one's attention to," comes to mean "take heed of, understand" in later Romance languages – OFr. *entendere*, Sp. *entender*, and It. *intendere* all mean "understand." But in French the semantic development did not stop there, and *entendre* in Modern French has the primary meaning "hear" (ousting OFr. *ouïr*, the legitimate heir of Lat. *audire*). Something similar may be going on in the domain of vision: in at least one case, a verb seems to have shifted from the realm of intellection to a possibly (if not completely) physical visual meaning, namely *recognize*, which derives from the Latin root *gno-* "know." Thus, although the paths of semantic change which I am describing do seem to be primarily one-way (concrete → abstract, or physical → mental), nonetheless some verbs may shift in the opposite direction along these same axes.

2.3.3 Smell, Taste, and Feel

In all Indo-European languages, the verb meaning "feel" in the sense of tactile sensation is the same as the verb indicating general sensory perception – Buck remarks on this general identity. It seems, furthermore, to be the case that sight is the sense most regularly differentiated from general perception, followed by hearing.[10] Even hearing sometimes falls under the rubric of a more general verb, e.g. Wel. *clywed* "perceive, hear" or Lat. *sentire* "feel, hear." Smell and taste frequently come under general sense perception (cf. Fr. *sentir* "feel, smell").

When smell and taste are differentiated from general tactile sensation, the verbs indicating these senses often derive from specific physical sensations (a sweet smell, a bad taste) or from aspects of the physical act of perception. Thus Eng. *smell* has been tentatively linked by Pokorny (1959–1969) with *smoulder*, perhaps via a meaning of "vapor" or "steam." Eng. *reek* is cognate with Ger. *rauchen* "smoke." Br. *c'hwez* means either "breath" or "smell"; the derived verbs *c'hwesa* (objective) and *kaout c'hwez* (subjective; lit. "take/get a breath or smell") mean "smell." (Cognate are Wel. *chwyth* "breath" and Ir. *setim* "blow.") Lat. *fragrare* "to be fragrant" gives Fr. *flairer* "to smell out, like a dog at a scent." The basic Indo-European "smell" root seems probably to have been *od-*, as inherited in Lat. *odor, odefacere/olfacere*, and in Gk *ózo:* (substantive *odmé:*). But the Modern Greek verb *mirízo:* meaning "smell" derives rather from Classical *murízo:* "to anoint, to perfume."

Taste may possibly have had a basic Indo-European root *g'eus-*, whose Greek and Latin descendents (*geúomai, gustare*) mean "taste," while the Germanic and Celtic cognates mean "try" or "choose" (Goth. *kiusan* "try," OE *ceosan* "choose"), and the Indo-Iranian cognates mean "enjoy" (Skt *juṣ-*). The direction of semantic development is not, however, clear; the Indo-European root could have meant "try" rather than "taste." English *taste* comes from a Latin root meaning "touch," also giving us *tactile; taste* comes via French, which still preserves *tâter* "to touch or try." Other Indo-European words for taste come from good (or sweet) tastes: OE *swaecc* "taste" is cognate with Wel. *chwaeth* "taste" and *chweg* "sweet" (Br. *c'houek*). Gk *chumós* (objective) and *cheûsis* (subjective) come from the same root as *chéo:* "pour" – *chumós*, in fact, basically means "juice."

A particularly interesting case is Lat. *sapere*, meaning both "be wise, know" and "taste." The sense of taste is here evidently connected not merely with general experience or perception, but with *mental* experience as well. The French verb *savoir* (from *sapere*) has only the sense of "know," but the noun *saveur* (from the Latin noun *sapor*, alongside *sapere*) means "savor, taste."

In general, the target domains of smell and taste are not the intellectual domain of *savoir*, however. The sense of smell has few abstract or mental connotations, although bad smell is used in English to indicate bad character or dislikeable mental characteristics ("he's a stinker," or "that idea stinks"), while the active verb *smell* may indicate detection of such characteristics ("I smell something fishy about this deal"). Taste, however, is a physical sense which seems universally to be linked to personal likes and dislikes in the mental world. Lat. *gustis* and Fr. *goût*, like Eng. *taste*, may indicate a "taste" in clothing or art as well as in food.

Finally, the sense of touch is not only linked with general sense perception, but is also closely tied to emotional "feeling." Thus, although there are specific words meaning "emotion" or "mental state" in many Indo-European languages, it is most commonly the case that a given language has at least one basic "emotional-feeling" word which comes from the domain of physical feeling. Thus, Lat. *sentire* indicates both physical and mental feeling, and Gk *páscho:* meant physical suffering before developing a sense of general (mental or physical) experience. Celtic and Germanic likewise show general homonymy in these two areas: Eng. *feel* (and its German cognates), Wel. *teimlo*, OIr. *cetbuid* and *mothugud*, are all both physical and mental. An interesting shift from one domain to the other is Gk *aísthe:ma* (from *aisthánomai* "perceive"), which went from a Classical Greek sense of "object of perception" (hence the English word *aesthetic*) to a Modern Greek meaning of "feeling, emotion."

2.4 The structure of our metaphors of perception

The next question, naturally, is what unifying pattern can be seen in the network of semantic changes described in the previous section. Further, are the link-ups between physical senses and mental states (or activities) motivated? Why is vision connected with intellection, rather than with obedience/heedfulness or with personal "taste"? Thus, I will next undertake an explication of the larger metaphorical structure which is the context of these individual metaphors and meaning shifts.

2.4.1 The objective and intellectual mental domain
The objective, intellectual side of our mental life seems to be regularly linked with the sense of vision, although other senses (as will be discussed below) occasionally take on intellectual meanings as well. There are major similarities in our general linguistic treatments of vision and intellection.

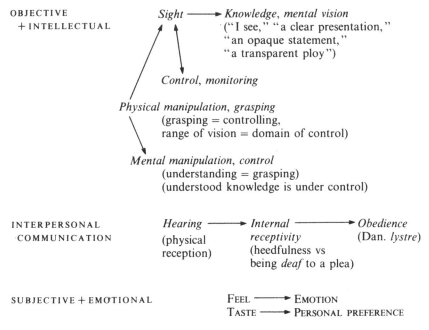

OBJECTIVE
+ INTELLECTUAL

Sight ────▶ *Knowledge, mental vision*
("I see," "a clear presentation,"
"an opaque statement,"
"a transparent ploy")

Control, monitoring

Physical manipulation, grasping
(grasping = controlling,
range of vision = domain of control)

Mental manipulation, control
(understanding = grasping)
(understood knowledge is under control)

INTERPERSONAL
COMMUNICATION

Hearing ────▶ *Internal* ────────▶ *Obedience*
(physical   *receptivity*   (Dan. *lystre*)
reception)   (heedfulness vs
                 being *deaf* to a plea)

SUBJECTIVE + EMOTIONAL

FEEL ────▶ EMOTION
TASTE ────▶ PERSONAL PREFERENCE

Diagram 1   The structure of our metaphors of perception

As shown in diagram 1, physical manipulation and touching is a source domain for words meaning both sight (visually picking out a stimulus) and mental data-manipulation (grasping a fact = understanding). Thus, a word such as *discern*, which comes from a root meaning "separate," now means both "catch sight of" and "mentally realize." Grasping and manipulation are evidence of control: which facts do we have under control, the facts we understand ("have a hold on," "have grasped") or those which we do not understand? Similarly, our visual picking out and monitoring of stimuli is evidence of control (our "scope" in English is our domain of control, whereas in Greek the word still belongs to the visual domain).

Thus, vision and intellection are viewed in parallel ways, partly (as I argued earlier) because of the focusing ability of our visual sense – the ability to pick out one stimulus at will from many is a salient characteristic of vision and of thought, but certainly not characteristic of any of the other physical senses except hearing. Even hearing is less consciously and readily focused than vision – I can literally move my eyes from one object to another, while it may require a good deal of effort to attend to one auditory stimulus among many (e.g., to the one conversation in which we are participating, rather than to the five others in the room, which are socially considered as background noise).

But most of all, vision is connected with intellection because it is our primary source of objective data about the world. Child-language studies (e.g. E. Clark 1976) have shown that visual features are among the most marked in children's early discrimination of one category from another; and, as mentioned earlier, crosslinguistic studies of evidentials show that direct visual evidence is considered the strongest and most reliable source of data. This is reasonable, since vast numbers of objects in daily life do not give forth auditory stimuli, and it would be impossible for the child to constantly taste, smell, or touch every object to be encountered. As the child matures, social understanding of appropriate distance also develops; it may not merely be dangerous to touch or taste, it may be socially inappropriate to get that close. Vision gives us data from a distance. This ability to reach out is a significant parallel between vision and intellection, since the objective and intellectual domain is understood as being an area of personal *distance*, in contrast to the intimacy or closeness of the subjective and emotional domain (we may keep someone *at a distance* by keeping the conversation intellectual; and if we feel too *close* to someone, then maybe we can no longer be objective about that person).

Vision is also identical for different people – that is to say, two people who stand in the same place are generally understood to see the same thing. (We must take into account our *point of view*, which means that if you are NOT standing in the same place then you may not see the same thing – but note that this is assuming that without the effect of a different location, the perception would be identical.) Identity across people is a highly objective characteristic – a further reason why vision resembles our folk understanding of our intellectual processes as objective. It is particularly interesting to note the behavior of languages such as French or German, which divide knowledge into objective (factual knowledge "that" something is true, or "how-to" knowledge) versus personal/experiential knowledge (acquaintance with a person, for example). So far as I can tell, the kind of knowledge expressed by Fr. *connaître* or Ger. *kennen* is not the sort of thing that speakers can say "I see" about, while much of the knowledge describable by *savoir* or *wissen* falls into the "I see" domain.

The vision/intellection metaphor is thoroughly alive today and highly structured; in modern English, much of the detailed vocabulary of our visual domain can be used to structure the description of our intellectual processes. Thus, just as a physical object may be opaque or transparent (and impedes vision or not, accordingly), likewise an argument or a proposition may be "(crystal)-clear," "opaque," "transparent," "muddy," or "murky" to our mental vision. We may "shed some light" on a problem which was particularly mysterious until that moment; and an intelligent idea or person is "bright," or even "brilliant," presumably because of a tendency to "illuminate" in this manner (for people who were previously "in the dark"). Someone who concentrates on one particular set of issues, to the exclusion of related (and/or more important) questions, is said to have "tunnel vision"; intellectual "breadth" of vision would be the opposite. *Clearsighted, sharp-eyed,* and *blind* all have applications to the facility of a person's mental observations as well as to physical perception.

"Vision" applies to the religious or spiritual as well as to the intellectual realm, though in a special sense, which is rather more restricted in modern usage than our visual metaphor for intellection. In the older Indo-European cultures, physical and spiritual "vision" were so strongly connected that physical blindness was considered to be a necessary concomitant of the highest level of internal (intellectual and spiritual) vision; the great prototypical mythical bards and prophets were blind, and ordinary bards often composed in darkness to remove the outer visual stimuli and allow themselves to focus on the inner vision. But in these cultures, it must be emphasized, the spiritual realm was not considered to be a purely subjective and personal domain at all – rather the reverse; it was objective and real, just like the world of daily life, but *hidden* from our everyday mortal sight, and hence only to be seen by those with appropriate inner vision. Nor was there a separation between the intellectual and the religious – bards filled the position of historians, and prophets were political advisors. Direct religious "vision" (or revelation) was considered not as a variable and subjective mode of knowledge, but as a factual revelation of another level of reality. Modern usage of words such as religious "vision" has become tinged with a coloring of personal hallucination, at least in the world of rationalists; but it is important to remember that spiritual vision started off as a generally accepted part of the intellectual world.

2.4.2   The communicative and subjective internal self

Hearing, it is true, shares some of vision's channeling characteristics, though not the voluntary on–off control which eye closure gives to vision, nor the channeling by physical movement of the sensory organ itself – auditory "channeling" is mainly a mental activity, while visual channeling is largely physical. Hearing is also, like vision, useful at a distance. But (as previously mentioned) not everything emits auditory stimuli; sight is a far more generally useful sense for data gathering. The function of hearing *par excellence* is, of course, linguistic communication; and since it is our major communicative pathway, it is also our major means of intellectual and emotional influence on each other. As linguistically capable beings, we have no need to constantly resort to physical pushes and pulls to influence other speakers of our language; we can do so in a far more sophisticated and effective manner via the vocal organs and the auditory sense-channel. Thus it is natural that physical auditory reception should be linked with heedfulness and internal "receptivity" ("not being *deaf* to someone's plea") and hence also to obedience (as seen in the *k'leu-s-descendents which mean "obey," like Dan. *lystre*). Internal reception of ideas, in the sense of *understanding* what is heard, is certainly often connected with the vocabulary of physical hearing. Not only do we have modern English usages such as *I hear you* (meaning "I understand you," and in particular "I am trying to put myself in your emotional place"), but we have already noted the semantic shift in the opposite direction on the part of Fr. *entendre* (although *entendre* now means simply "hear," idiomatic usages such as the reflexive *s'entendre* in its meaning of "understand each other, get along with each other," together with other relics of the older meaning such as *malentendu* "misunderstanding" or *entendu* "heard" OR "understood/OK," persist as evidence of this shift). But readiness to internally receive and understand implies also a readiness to subject oneself to the influence of the speaker's content – and hence perhaps a readiness to further respond in the way desired (e.g., to obey if a command is involved).

That hearing and heedfulness are deeply linked in Indo-European tradition can be further confirmed by a glance at the *Iliad*. An analysis of the use of *klúo* in book I of the *Iliad* shows that it is consistently used to mean "be receptive to, take heed of," and in fact (already in this early text) has primarily gone beyond its original physical meaning of "hear." I was unable to find a single instance referring simply to physical sound reception (the verb *aío*: "perceive or hear," is used in this sense).

Common usage of *klúo:* in the *Iliad* is well exemplified by Chryses' plea to Apollo (I,37) *klûthí meu Argurótox'* "Hear me, O Silver-bowed one". Chryses naturally does not mean simply physical hearing; one might even argue that (as seen elsewhere in the Homeric corpus) the gods are generally supposed to see and hear all sorts of distant things, without any special mortal appeals. Rather, Chryses means to ask for Apollo's favourable *reception* of his plea; for the god "not to be deaf" to his prayer. And in fact this entails Apollo not merely agreeing, but acting – hence "hear me" really means "*do* as I ask." Such a reading is confirmed by the closure of Chryses' prayer: *toû d'éklue Phoîbos Apóllo:n* ("And Phoibos Apollo heard him"), which is immediately followed by the statement that Apollo came down from Olympos and shot arrows of pestilence at the Greeks (to punish them as Chryses had asked him to). When, later in book I, Agamemnon returns Chryses' daughter in an attempt to save his army from the pestilence, Chryses again prays to Apollo, this time in favor of the Greeks: the opening sequence is identical to that of his previous prayer, as is the closing. In this prayer, however, is an even more interesting sequence. Chryses says to Apollo, "Even as you heard me before when I prayed (*e:mèn de:pot' emeû páros éklues euxaménoio*),...*so now fulfill* me this desire: ward the loathly pestilence from the Greeks." The equation between "*hearing*" and fulfilling a prayer is strikingly evident. A final example of equal interest occurs in the argument between Achilles and Agamemnon. Athene, seizing Achilles by the hair, holds him back from fighting Agamemnon and advises him to keep the combat verbal rather than physical. Achilles responds by stating that Athene and Hera have to be obeyed, and adds (I,218) *Hós ke theoîs epipeíthe:tai, mála t'ékluon autoû* ("Whoso *obeys* the gods, to him do they gladly *listen*"). He means, of course, that the gods *grant* the prayers of obedient mortals – there is an exchange wherein the gods will do your will if you have previously done theirs. He uses the verb *klúo:* "hear" to express favorable reception and granting of prayers.

The link between physical hearing and obeying or heeding – between physical and internal receptivity or reception – may well, in fact, be universal, rather than merely Indo-European. A partial examination of a Hebrew Old Testament concordance[11] alongside an English translation shows large numbers of instances where the basic Hebrew root meaning "hear" (s-m-ʕ) is used to mean "obey" or "understand" or "listen/heed," and in fact is often translated into English by one of these other English words. Examples (instances of the relevant Hebrew verb are italicized in the translated text):

Jer. 22:21   I spoke to you...but you said "I will not *listen.*"
(God is here chastising humans for *disobedience.*)
Zech. 7:12   And they made their hearts like flint so that they would not *hear* the law and the words which the Lord of hosts had sent.
(Note: they don't just stop their *ears* (as in 7:11), they harden their hearts against *internal* reception and obedience.)
Gen. 11:7   Let us confuse their language, so that they may not *understand* each other's speech.
(Note: This is God speaking, in the Tower of Babel story. He is not intending to stop their hearing by affecting their ears, but rather their internal "hearing" – understanding – by confusing their language. But the Hebrew text has the verb "hear.")

It is probably the case, then, that hearing is universally connected with the internal as well as the external aspects of speech reception. Inasmuch as speech is the communication of information or of other matter for the intellect, hearing as well as sight is connected with intellectual processing. It is thus not surprising that "I see" should mean "I understand," but that Fr. *entendre* "hear" should also etymologically be connected with understanding. But hearing is connected with the specifically communicative aspects of understanding, rather than with intellection at large. (It would be a novelty for a verb meaning "hear" to develop a usage meaning "know" rather than "understand," whereas such a usage is common for verbs meaning "see.") In a larger context, hearing is also considered to represent the kind of internal receptiveness to the speaker's intentions which might subsequently lead to compliance with the speaker's requests – i.e., to heedfulness and obedience.

We have said that the sense of smell has fewer and less deep metaphorical connections with the mental domain than the other senses. Taste, however, is deeply linked with our internal self, and is used to represent our personal likes and dislikes or "tastes." And the vocabulary of touch and tactile sensation is generally used for emotional sensations of all types – we can be emotionally "wounded," "stroked," "touched (to the heart)," and so forth. Why should these physical senses carry *these* particular abstract meanings, rather than other ones?

As previously mentioned, distance is connected with objectivity and intellect, closeness with subjectivity, intimacy, and emotion. Vision and hearing are distant senses, while taste and touch require actual physical contact with the thing sensed. (Of course sound waves and light waves must actually reach our eyes and ears for sensation to take place; but the object "giving off" the stimuli may be distant.) Taste is a sense which is in fact not only "close" (in that we actually ingest the sensed object) but proverbially subjective in its variability across people – "one man's meat is another man's poison," and *de gustibus non est disputandum.* Personal likes and dislikes in other domains – clothing, music, friends – are equally variable and equally subjective, and are thus well represented in terms of the vocabulary of physical taste.

Touch is intersubjectively variable as well; pleasure and pain responses differ hugely. Regarding tactile data input, we may remember the story of the blind men and the elephant as an embodiment of the crucial difference between the intimate, non-general, non-objective input of touch, and the more distant, objective, general data derived from vision. This story captures in a nutshell the reasons why our sense of touch is not connected with intellection, but with emotion. Further reasons are (as previously stated) the actual impossibility of using touch for general data-gathering, both because of possible danger in many cases and (more often) because of the social inappropriateness of such an intimacy as physical contact. But perhaps the most basic factor of all is that discussed by Kurath (1921): in particular for our sense of touch (and for the accompanying general physical senses such as pain perception or thermal and kinesthetic perception) there is not a simple and tidy way to divide physical perception from emotion. Physical pain of any serious nature is bound to make the subject unhappy emotionally, and physical pleasure or well-being certainly promotes a cheerful emotional state; the psyche likewise affects corporal sensation, to such an extent that physicians acknowledge their inability to keep psychic and somatic health rigorously divided. None of the other senses, limited as they are to perception of much more specific data than the agglomeration of physical perception which we connect with "feeling," has such a general correlation with our internal emotional state, and hence such a strong perceptual motivation for a general metaphorical mapping onto the semantics of the psyche.[12]

2.5   Conclusions

The vocabulary of physical perception thus shows systematic metaphorical connections with the vocabulary of internal self and internal sensations. These connections are not random correspondences, but highly motivated links between parallel or *analogous* areas of physical and internal sensation. Nor are the correspondences isolated; Lakoff and Johnson, who correctly link up individual parts of our physical and mental vocabularies (such as understanding = grasping, or knowing = seeing) in their analysis of metaphor, do not yet notice that these are parts of a larger system of the kind which they would refer to as a conceptual metaphor. (That is, this metaphor involves our conceptualizing one whole area of experience in terms of another.) The internal self is pervasively understood in terms of the bodily external self, and is hence described by means of vocabulary drawn (either synchronically or diachronically) from the physical domain. Some aspects of the instantiation of this metaphor may be fairly common crossculturally, if not universal – for example, the connection between vision and knowledge – while others (in particular, less general aspects such as the choice of the vital organ which is thought to be the seat of emotion) may vary a good deal between cultures. (Matisoff [1978] is a fascinating study of the culturally understood link-ups between physical and abstract vocabulary in the Tibeto-Burman family.)

It should be reiterated that our models of our internal world are not always consistent, and in particular that we have multiple, apparently inconsistent mappings of our physical selves onto our internal selves. Sometimes consistency emerges from such apparently inconsistent mappings. For example, it appears inconsistent to describe the acquisition of knowledge both as seeing and as grasping; but when we notice that seeing is itself talked about in the vocabulary of grasping and object manipulation, we can see that there is some deeper regularity. (It is still unclear, however, whether knowledge is talked about as vision, vision as grasping, and hence – transitively – knowledge as grasping; or whether knowledge and vision are independently treated as grasping.)[13]

Such large-scale conceptual metaphors are of the highest importance for synchronic and diachronic semantic analysis. Through a historical analysis of "routes" of semantic change, it is possible to elucidate synchronic semantic connections between lexical domains; similarly,

connections are across one point in time, namely the present — not over a period of time

synchronic connections may help clarify reasons for shifts of meaning in past linguistic history.

Given our understanding of this particular metaphorical system and the paths of meaning-change mapped out by it, let us now return to the "puzzles" with which I began this chapter. The connections between hearing and obedience and between grasping and understanding have been discussed in some detail already. Now, given a mapping of the physical domain onto our mental domain, we can elucidate the other puzzles as well. The *way* in *anyway* and in Italian *tuttavia* historically comes from the physical domain. But logical structures and conversational structures are at least partly understood in terms of physical traveling and motion. An argument or a conversation follows or covers some particular path through the mental areas it traverses. Thus we say "That was off the track of the argument," "The professor guided his students through the maze of tax law," "They didn't let him get very far into the subject," or "Where were we?" *Anyway* presumably means "by any mental or conversational path we take, we will reach this conclusion."

The historical connection between the lexicon of physical similarity and that of probability or likelihood (the *like–likely* link-up) is a more complex case. We assess similarity or likeness not merely between objects or entities, but between whole situations. Not merely physical likeness is involved; likeness at a more abstract mental level is also referred to in terms of physical likeness. In fact, if you say to me "John and Mary are alike," I cannot tell without further data at what level you are comparing them. Further, our Pavlovian reflexes tell us that we can reason from similar situations to probable similar results. In earlier English usage, it was possible to say "He is *like* to die," meaning what we would now say as "He is *likely* to die." If a person's appearance and situation *resemble* those of a person about to die, then (so far as we can tell) that person is more *likely* to die than someone whose appearance and situation are different. Thus physical resemblance and probable future fate are interconnected phenomena, at least in our folk understanding. (Compare modern English usages such as "It *looks like* Joe will be going to New York" vs "It *looks like* it's stormy out right now.")

These are simply two more cases of apparently whimsical meaning-shifts which fit neatly into the larger systematic framework that I have laid out above, using English perception-verbs as my case in point. If we are willing to look at such large-scale, systematic historical connections between domains of meaning, it becomes evident that not all of semantic change is as whimsical and perverse as has often been assumed. True, prediction of any individual change remains impossible and seems unlikely to become possible in the future. Phonological change and morphological change cannot be predicted on an individual basis either, so surely no one expects specific-case predictions for semantic or syntactic change. However, in many semantic domains it seems possible to determine what would be natural as opposed to unnatural directions of change, just as in phonology we know that voiced stops would be likely to devoice in final position or to become fricatives in intervocalic position, rather than the other way around.

Semantic fields and semantic changes are then possibly as systematically structured as is the phonological domain, although semantic structuring seems frequently impossible to describe in terms of objective features. If I know that one perception verb in a given language is connected with the domain of internal self (if, for example, I find that "see" frequently comes to mean "know" historically, or is used to mean "know" synchronically), then I am far less surprised to find that "hear" comes to refer to understanding or obedience in that language, or that "taste" is connected with personal likes and dislikes. In phonology, if I find that *b* and *d* are subject to final devoicing, I will expect to find that *g* is devoiced finally as well. And, just as in phonology I will expect *g* to devoice to *k* and *b* to *p* (rather than the other way around, *g* to *p* and *b* to *k*), in semantic change I will expect to find sight systematically linked with intellection and touch *come to* with emotion, rather than the other way around, or rather than sight with *expect* obedience and hearing with emotion. Internal structuring of, and *certain* correspondences between, semantic domains are equally regular – as *connections* discussed above, it is not an accident that a *clear* statement aids mental vision while an *opaque* one impedes it, or that a *bright* idea sheds mental *illumination*, rather than causing obfuscation of the issues.

There is coherent, regular structuring within the metaphorical system of interconnections between semantic domains. But until change directions are systematically examined in the area of meaning, it will be impossible to tell how irregular or how regular meaning-change really is; further, such investigation will be fruitless, unless done against the backdrop of our synchronic structuring of the domains in question. Such examination of semantic change has only recently begun to be carried out. For the domain of perception verbs, now that we have examined the system, we have some idea what semantic changes would be "regular" or "normal," and what changes would be abnormal. Phonological change, after all, looked irregular until the relevant parameters were examined and isolated by the Neogrammarians; and it seems fair to suppose that the relevant parameters in semantics are far more complex (not being constrained by limiting factors as narrow as the physiology of speech) than those of phonology.[14] The fact is, then, that we need to continue investigating the *least* surprising etymologies we can find, like *see > know*; the boring semantic histories are really the most interesting ones for our current state of research, because they allow us a more transparent view of the general principles underlying them.

3 Modality[1]

3.1 Introduction

In the preceding chapter I have argued that a pervasive and coherently structured system of metaphors underlies our tendency to use vocabulary from the external (sociophysical) domain in speaking of the internal (emotional and psychological) domain. Historically, this metaphorical system has guided the course of numerous semantic changes; and synchronically, it is represented by numerous polysemous words and extended "abstract" uses of physical-world vocabulary. In this chapter I shall examine in detail one particular vocabulary domain which shows synchronic ambiguity between the external and internal worlds: modality.

The ambiguity of modal expressions between "root" (or deontic)[2] and epistemic senses has long been recognized. Linguists have characterized as *root* those meanings which denote real-world obligation, permission, or ability (as in example [1]); and as *epistemic* those which denote necessity, probability, or possibility in reasoning (as in [2]).

(1) John *must* be home by ten; Mother won't let him stay out any later.
(2) John *must* be home already; I see his coat.

this differentiation is crosscultural

This ambiguity is not peculiar to English; indeed, there is an evident crosslinguistic tendency for lexical items to be ambiguous between these two sets of senses. Many unrelated languages (Indo-European, Semitic, Philippine, Dravidian, Mayan, and Finno-Ugric, among others[3]) are alike in having some set of predicates which carry both the root and epistemic modal meanings, as English modal verbs do. Frequently this set of predicates is a relatively small, morphosyntactically distinct set, also as in English.[4] Such a crosslinguistic correlation encourages us to search for a broader motivation in the linking of these two apparently disparate semantic domains.

There is strong historical, sociolinguistic, and psycholinguistic evidence

traditional view

for viewing the epistemic use of modals as an extension of a more basic root meaning, rather than viewing the root sense as an extension of the epistemic one, or both as sub-sets of some more general superordinate sense. Historically, the English modals developed from non-modal meanings (such as physical strength or force, e.g. OE *magan* "be strong, be able") to "deontic" *(root)* modal meanings, and later still broadened to include the epistemic readings as well (see Ehrman 1966; Shepherd 1981). Shepherd's work on Antiguan Creole gives some evidence that creoles first develop their expression of root modality before going on to extend that expression fully to the epistemic domain. And studies of child language (Kuczaj and Daly 1979; Shepherd 1981) have revealed that children acquire the deontic senses of modal verbs earlier than the epistemic ones. Given these facts alongside the crosslinguistic pervasiveness of the ambiguity, it seems reasonable to suppose that the link between the two senses is not a chance artifact of the vagaries of one language's past historical development.

? deontic : physical sense of the verbs owes before the more abstract (dealing w/ reason)

Past historical changes in this domain, then, were shaped by a general semantic linkage which probably has inherent psycholinguistic motivation. My proposal is that root-modal meanings are extended to the epistemic domain precisely because we generally use the language of the external world to apply to the internal mental world, which is metaphorically structured as parallel to that external world. Thus we view our reasoning processes as being subject to compulsions, obligations, and other modalities, just as our real-world actions are subject to modalities of the same sort. Nor is modality the only area where we treat our epistemic world as analogous to the sociophysical world: setting aside extensions of physical perception verbs to epistemic perception ("I see"), it is generally true that we treat the causality in reasoning processes in terms of the causality of events and actions. An examination of speech-act verbs, adverbial elements, causal and coordinate conjunctions, and *if–then* conditionals will show that all of these classes of linguistic entities can be applied to the epistemic world as well as to the real world.

The present study will thus argue that modal verbs do not have two separate unrelated senses, but rather show an extension of the basic root-sense to the epistemic domain – an extension which is strongly motivated by the surrounding linguistic system. It must be noted that previous analysts have looked at modal verbs' ambiguity quite differently. Indeed, much recent linguistic work seems to treat English modal verbs as essentially cases of homonymy rather than ambiguity, tacitly assuming that (whatever the historical development may have been) epistemic and root modality are synchronically unrelated (see R. Lakoff 1972a; Lyons 1977). Root-modal meanings are often treated as lexical predicates involving force or obligation, while epistemic readings are treated as combinations of logical operators. For the reasons given above, such an analysis is inherently implausible. And yet it would be tantalizingly insufficient to simply assert the semantic closeness between root- and epistemic-modal senses (as do Steele *et al.* 1981). Given that (as Palmer [1986] observes) the two sets of meanings are highly distinct and objectively have little in common, such an assertion essentially reduces to the fact of frequent polysemy relationships, and begs the question as to the reason for such relationships. We need an analysis of root and epistemic modality which will in some way make natural their clear, close, crosslinguistic semantic relationship. The framework laid out in chapter 2 suggests the direction for a reanalysis of the semantics of English modals which will relate root and epistemic senses in a motivated way, showing how the root/epistemic polysemy is interrelated with other semantic and pragmatic polysemy/ambiguity patterns in the language.

I shall begin, therefore, by putting forward an analysis of root modality which I have chosen because it is readily extendable from the sociophysical to the epistemic domain. Given our understanding of mental "forces" in terms of real-world forces, this analysis of modal semantics can be mapped in a regular fashion onto the epistemic world. In the final section of this chapter, and in the following two chapters, I shall expand my analysis from the area of modality to propose a general understanding of a mapping from the sociophysical to the epistemic domain in the areas of causality, conjunction, and conditionality.

3.2   The root modals in English

One of the main obstacles to the evolution of a unified understanding of modality has been the fact that semantic analyses of root modality were not systematically relatable to logical necessity or probability. So we must choose our root-modal analysis with care, if we hope to make it mesh with epistemic modality. Talmy (1981, 1988) has suggested that the semantics of root modality is best understood in terms of force dynamics, that is in terms of our linguistic treatment of forces and barriers in general. Thus, for example, permitting (e.g. *may, let,* and *allow*) is an instance of taking away (or keeping away) a potentially present barrier. With *let* or *allow,* that barrier may be a physical one (as in [3]) or a social one (as in [4]); *may* seems more restricted to social permission in its sociophysical uses in modern English, although more general sociophysical uses preceded this use.

(3) The crack in the stone *let* the water flow through.
(4) I begged Mary to *let* me have another cookie.

Adopting Talmy's basic idea of viewing modality in terms of forces and barriers, I shall offer tentative force-dynamic analyses of all the root modals. My primary object will be to demonstrate subsequently that such analyses are possible and readily extendable to the epistemic domain, rather than to argue strongly for this specific set of analyses as they stand. It should be understood that I do not explicitly take my analyses from Talmy, except in the case of *may*, although they are clearly in the general spirit of his work. Further, he takes the purely physical level of force dynamics (e.g. a stone resisting water) as the most basic of all, while I prefer to view modality as basically referring to intentional, directed forces and barriers. Within the domain of intentional causality, I do feel (as Talmy does) that direct physical manipulation of the environment is more prototypical causality (and hence more prototypical modality) than is indirect or purely social manipulation (see Talmy 1976). But this work will not attempt to deal with the relative basicness of different kinds of real-world forces in our understanding of causation; rather, I shall simply propose a force-dynamic analysis of modality, with the understanding that I am referring to generalized sociophysical concepts of forces and barriers.[5]

May and *must* are perhaps the most clearly force-dynamic of the modals. Talmy's understanding of *may* in terms of a potential but absent barrier seems to me very reasonable, and can be viewed as a restatement of the standard analysis (e.g. "not require not") in terms of the more general concepts of forces and barriers. *Must* is equally readily understood as a compelling force directing the subject towards an act. Talmy would like to view *must* as a barrier restricting one's domain of action to a certain single act; and it is true that force or constraint would have the same physical result. But *must* has the force of an order to do something, a positive compulsion rather than a negative restriction. When I say "You must be home by ten," I indeed restrict my interlocutor's actions (or try to do so); but I do so *by* compelling the choice of some specific alternative. My attention is fixed not on the excluded alternatives but on the realization of the chosen alternative.[6]

Can is far more difficult to pin down than *may* or *must*. Talmy analyzes it as parallel to *may* in structure, but with less tendency for the absent barrier to return to its position. This solution would, of course, explain the frequent overlapping of *can* and *may*'s semantic territories, but I think the overlap is equally explicable in terms of a more intuitively satisfying definition of *can*. *Can* denotes positive ability on the part of the doer; *may* denotes lack of restriction on the part of someone else. The closest physical analogy to *can* would be *potential* force or energy (note the Latin-derived *potential*, referring to ability) – and perhaps the best force-dynamic characterization I can give for ability is to say that it is the human physical and social modality in terms of which we view potential energy in physics.

If we can permit ourselves an excursion into the simple physical domain for a moment, perhaps it will become clearer why *can* and *may* have such a tendency towards overlap. Let us view *can* as being the equivalent of a full gas tank in a car, and *may* as the equivalent of an open garage door. These two factors will exert certain similar influences on the situation: neither factor forces the car (or the driver) to travel a given path, and yet if either factor were reversed, then travel would be correspondingly restricted. The full tank is a positive enablement, while the open door is a negated restriction; yet the results are similar enough to allow a good deal of overlap in the larger force-dynamic schemata surrounding the two modalities. Thus it is not surprising to find *can* used to give permission: the remover of a barrier may even feel that in some sense this removal counts as an act of enablement. And, of course, it is also politer to (cooperatively) enable than to invoke your restrictive powers by overtly refraining from exercising them.[7]

We now come to *ought, have to*, and *need to*, which resemble *must* in denoting obligation or necessity; the difference is largely in the kind of obligation. *Ought* seems to be less strong than the others, and to have moral overtones, or at least to indicate that the obligation is one socially agreed upon between the imposer and the docr. *Have to* (as Talmy observes) has more of a meaning of being obliged by extrinsically imposed authority. And *need* implies that the obligation is imposed by something internal to the doer:

(5) $\left\{ \begin{array}{l} \text{I have} \\ \text{?I need} \end{array} \right\}$ to stay home, or Mom will get mad at me.

(6) $\left\{ \begin{array}{l} \text{You have} \\ \text{?You need} \end{array} \right\}$ to stay home, because I say so.

(7) $\left\{ \begin{array}{l} \text{I need} \\ \text{I have} \end{array} \right\}$ to stay home tonight to study for the test.

Either *need* or *have to* can be used in (7) because the obligation to study is an externally imposed one in one sense, and an internally imposed one in another (the student is free to neglect studying, though at the risk of failing the test). Talmy would prefer to analyze *have to, need to,* and *ought* as barriers; I have once again some doubts about this viewpoint. *Ought* especially seems to me to indicate a positive compulsion; but *need* also refers to the necessity for some specific action or object, rather than to restrictions on other possible actions. My own analysis of *must, ought, have to,* and *need to* is that they are different *kinds of forces. Must* has connotations of a directly applied and irresistible force, while *have to, ought,* and *need to* are resistible forces different with respect to their domains (social, moral) and/or sources of imposition (internal/external), as discussed above. Regarding the question of resistibility, note the contrasts in (8).

(8) $\left\{\begin{array}{l} \text{??I must} \\ \text{I have to} \\ \text{I need to} \\ \text{I ought to} \end{array}\right\}$ get this paper in, but I guess I'll go to the movies instead.

The basic point here is that within the limits of the meaning of each modal, anything that counts as a force can impose the relevant modality. Thus any internally rooted desire, lack, or compulsion can impose the modality *need*; and any social force which the subject participates in can count as conferring the obligation expressed in *ought.*

Finally, we come to the borderline modals *shall* and *will* (their distal forms, *should* and *would,* are highly modal). *Shall* and *will* can express simple futurity; but (as Palmer [1979][8] remarks with some surprise, after examining a large corpus) they don't usually do so in usage, despite grammar books. R. Lakoff (1972a) prefers to regard them as the strongest modals, on the grounds that the very strongest obligation or necessity is certainty of future action (see also Huddleston 1979). Certainly the *will* in examples such as (9) and (10) seems volitional rather than future pure and simple.

(9) All right, I'll do it; shake, mister.
(10) See if John will help you out. (= is he *willing*?)

Shall in my dialect (also in many of Palmer's examples) indicates the speaker or imposer (rather than the subject of the action) making him/herself responsible for the carrying out of the action. Thus (11) and

(12) have a sense that the speaker undertakes to see to it or to command that the action be done; while in (13) the law is viewed as doing this.[9]

(11) You *shall* go, I insist on it.
(12) If Mr Jones wants tickets for our concert, he shall have them.
(13) (The law decrees that) all citizens shall constantly carry violet parasols from 3/9/83 on. (the law = speaker)

The forces involved in (9)–(13) are those of volition and responsibility.

The purely future reading of *will* (*shall* has none in my dialect) seems to indicate not some force or barrier, but a completed path to an action or intention. How this fits into a force-dynamic analysis (if at all) is a difficult question. The one mistake which I can clearly identify in some past analyses is the idea that future *will* is always epistemic, and concerns future truth-value. Like all the modals except present-tense *shall*, *will* has both a root and an epistemic reading – contrast the real futurity in (14a) with the epistemic futurity of knowledge in (14b).

(14a) He will be home in three hours.
(14b) He will be home by now; I just saw the lights go on.

In (14b) the person is or is not at home, in the present; the *will* is of future discovery or verification – "if we check, we will find out that he is home." When an action is in the future, of course, its occurrence is automatically only knowable or verifiable in the future. But the epistemic use of *will* is an extension from the *will* of actual futurity to purely epistemic futurity: the actual event is not in the future, but only its verification. Note that so long as verification is future, the event can be past as easily as present – "future-perfect" forms are thus ambiguous between a root *will* (perfectivity in the future) and an epistemic *will* (future verification of perfectivity):

(15a) He will have completed his requirements by the end of this term – he will then be able to graduate.
(15b) He will have completed his requirements long ago, of course – I don't know why I'm bothering to check the records.

The distal[10] forms of the root modals express past or conditional modality; distance in either a temporal or a causal sequence is thus marked identically. *Could* expresses past or conditional ability, and *might* (in those dialects where it has a root sense) expresses a past or conditional absence of a barrier. *Ought to* and *must* have no morphologically distinct past forms: both of them can act as either present or past with respect to tense-sequencing in dependent clauses (e.g. "He thinks he can/ought to" vs "He thought he could/ought to"), but neither of them has an independent past or conditional form. *Should* has filled part of the distal slot for *ought to*; since *shall* is relatively rare, its distal form was perhaps freed to shift as needed within the modal system. It was a natural choice for this slot, since whatever a speaker is willing to assume responsibility for ("should") is also something the speaker might conditionally agree was morally appropriate or obligatory ("ought"). The pure past of *ought*, however, is usually represented by the periphrastic "be supposed to" form. *Must* is so specially an expression of direct force that it seems natural for it to lack a distal form; when a past form is required, *had to* is used, but its meaning is not quite a distal *must*. *Have to* and *need to* have past forms; but like all conjugated English verbs, their past forms are not conditionals in main clauses – *would have to* and *would need to* are the conditionals, except in *if*-clauses. Finally, *would* expresses the distal form of both the future *will* and volitional-force *will*. In general, whatever modal forces or barriers the present form of a modal verb expresses, the distal form of the verb will express those forces conditionally or in the past.

3.3   Epistemic modality as an extension of root modality

3.3.1   Past unified analyses of modality

Given the tentative beginnings of a general analysis of root modality in terms of sociophysical forces, barriers, and paths of different kinds, let us now explore the results of transferring this view to the epistemic domain. We would like to achieve a unified analysis of modality. One direction taken by past "unified" analyses (e.g. Kratzer 1977) has been essentially to subsume the root meanings of the modals under very general epistemic readings; thus root *can* comes to refer to logical compatibility between a person's (or the world's) state and some event, while root *must* refers to logical necessity of the occurrence of some event, given the state of the world. Even if analyses such as Kratzer's did not have the drawback of entirely ignoring the intentionality inherent in root modality, they would still fail to motivate the attested historical and developmental progression from root to epistemic, rather than the other direction. A slightly more promising line of explanation is that suggested in passing by Lyons (1977): namely that epistemic uses of the modals result from our understanding the logical necessity of a proposition in terms of the forces which give rise to the sociophysical necessity of the corresponding event in the real

doesn't work

world.[11] But this too falls down when closely examined: in uttering the attested example (16), the speaker did not really mean that somehow the proposition must be true because some real-world causes have brought about the relevant state of affairs, but rather that he was obliged to *conclude* that it was true because the available informational premises caused him to reason thus.

(16) (looks at nametag) "You must be Seth Sweetser's sister."

Nonetheless, Lyons' idea is a more useful starting point than any of the analyses which assume the existence of a superordinate modality that has deontic and epistemic sub-classes. Ehrman's (1966) attempt to find superordinate "core meanings" for the modals resulted in some extremely vague analyses, and still left her with two separate meanings for *may*.

Boyd and Thorne (1969) and Tregidgo (1982)[12] in different ways propose analyses which allow epistemic modals to get readings referring to the necessity or permissibility of the act of stating, while root modals refer to the necessity or possibility of the event described in the statement. This is getting closer, but is still not quite accurate, since in fact epistemic modals don't apply to our acts of stating, but to our acts of induction or deduction. Thus (16) does not express the speaker's compulsion to *state* that the addressee has a certain identity, but his compulsion to *conclude* that this is the case. Phrases like "I must say" or "I must tell you," which genuinely express modality applied to the act of speaking, have a completely different meaning from epistemic modals. (Later, in section 3.4, I will discuss senses of the modals which seem to relate more directly to the speech-act domain.)

Finally, Antinucci and Parisi (1971) have suggested that *belief* figures in the semantics of epistemic modals. Thus they propose that *must* has two readings analyzable as in (17) and (18):

(17) You must come home. (deontic)

CAUSE $\left\{ \begin{array}{c} X \\ \text{Speaker} \end{array} \right\}$ (BIND (YOU COME HOME))

(18) You must have been home last night. (epistemic)

CAUSE (X) (BIND (BELIEVE (SPEAKER) (YOU BE HOME)))

Restated in English, this analysis proposes that epistemic modality binds the speaker to believe the proposition, while deontic modality binds the subject to do the action expressed in the proposition. Antinucci and Parisi are clearly on the right track. I would prefer to talk about conclusions rather than beliefs, since conclusions are precisely that class of beliefs which we are bound to adopt or not to adopt by our reasoning processes. Also, we shall see (in the next two sections of this chapter) that an analysis of modality need not have separate formal-semantic structures for root and epistemic modals; we need not view *must* as semantically ambiguous between CAUSE (BIND()) and CAUSE (BIND (BELIEVE())), but rather perhaps as semantically ambiguous between our sociophysical understanding of force and some mapping of that understanding onto the domain of reasoning. This makes explicit the identity of the CAUSE and BIND predicates; it is not the application of some general idea of binding to the area of belief which is at stake, so much as our comprehension of belief structure in terms of a basically sociophysical idea of forcing. The polysemy of the modals, then, may lie rather in the presence or absence of a metaphorical mapping than in the presence or absence of a single feature making the sense more specific.[13]

Further, it is not necessary for the speaker and hearer, or imposer and imposee of the modality, to be explicitly present in the semantic structure of the modals. (If they are present in semantics, then modals are ambiguous between potentially infinite numbers of structures; but in fact, these participants are pragmatically identified – see section 3.3.3.)

Antinucci and Parisi do not address the question of the semantics of the general predicate *bind*: what does it mean (other than *must*), and why should it happen to apply equally well to real events and to reasoning processes? (There is some tacit assumption here that events and conclusions can be treated alike.) I trust that the rudimentary analysis of root modality in the preceding section has given some idea of the elements of my proposed general analysis of modality; in the next section, I shall attempt to explore and then motivate the link-up between real-world modality and epistemic modality.

3.3.2   *Root modality applied to the epistemic world*

If root modality is viewed as referring specifically to permission giving or to social duty, for example, there would appear to be little chance of extending such an analysis to epistemic modality. The *may* of permission granting and the *may* of possibility seem unconnected, since there is no permission granter in the world of reasoning. The connection is particularly unlikely if our analysis of the epistemic-modal senses is based on an objective understanding of logical certainty or possibility; but there is every reason to reject this viewpoint. I am fully in agreement with Palmer (1986) when he says that the so-called *alethic* modalities of abstract necessity and possibility (however useful in formal logic) play a negligible role in natural-language semantics.[14] Palmer further argues that the English modal verbs in their epistemic senses largely express speaker judgment. I have argued above in favor of a similar position.[15] If this is so, then in order to motivate the root–epistemic polysemy of the English modals, we need to find a motivated semantic connection between the epistemic domain of reasoning and judgment and the domain of external sociophysical modality.

The preceding chapter has already argued that our linguistic system shows pervasive evidence of a metaphorical understanding of our internal intellectual and psychological states in terms of our external selves. This evidence gives us a motivating background against which to set a more specific metaphorical mapping between epistemic and root modality. Given that the epistemic world is understood in terms of the sociophysical world, we can see why general sociophysical potentiality, and specifically social permission, should be the sociophysical modality chosen as analogous to possibility in the world of reasoning.[16] *May* is an absent potential barrier in the sociophysical world, and the epistemic *may* is the force-dynamically parallel case in the world of reasoning. The meaning of epistemic *may* would thus be that there is no barrier to the speaker's process of reasoning from the available premises to the conclusion expressed in the sentence qualified by *may*. My claim, then, is that an epistemic modality is metaphorically viewed as that real-world modality which is its closest parallel in force-dynamic structure.

The above paragraph is not intended to imply that physical, social, and epistemic barriers have something objectively in common, at however abstract a level. My idea is rather that our *experience* of these domains shares a limited amount of common structure, which is what allows a successful metaphorical mapping between the relevant aspects of the three domains. The mapping itself, then, further structures our understanding of the more abstract domains in terms of our (more directly experientially based) understanding of the more concrete domains. Since it is an essential feature of metaphor to map a concept onto another concept from a distinct domain, it is not possible that every aspect of the source domain can be mapped onto some aspect of the target domain. It has been suggested elsewhere (Sweetser 1988; Brugman and Lakoff 1988) that certain abstract and topological aspects of semantic structure, which we have termed *image-schematic structure*, are the aspects which must be preserved across metaphorical mappings. In the present context, one might schematically represent the image-schematic structure of *may* as something like the following diagram (representing a potential barrier which is not actually in place):

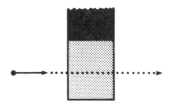

The shared topological structure intended to be portrayed in this diagram would include some of the following observations:

1.   In both the sociophysical and the epistemic worlds, *nothing prevents* the occurrence of whatever is modally marked with *may*; the chain of events is not obstructed.

2.   In both the sociophysical and epistemic worlds, there is some background understanding that if things were different, something *could* obstruct the chain of events. For example, permission or other sociophysical conditions could change; and added premises might make the reasoner reach a different conclusion.

This assumes that a basic causal event-structure is mapped from our understanding of social and physical causality onto our understanding of our reasoning processes. Once such a mapping is assumed to exist, it is clearly natural to map the meaning of *may* onto epistemic possibility, and not (for example) onto epistemic certainty, because there is some very general topological structure shared by the two senses of *may*. Using terminology borrowed from Fauconnier (1985), I would claim that epistemic possibility is the epistemic *counterpart* of root-modal *may*.

We may also here recall that there is broader evidence (see chapter 1) to support the hypothesis that our reasoning processes are metaphorically modelled as a journey through space; in this journey, physical obstacles are part of the landscape. Thus, we could say "This fact *blocks* me from reaching that conclusion." This is another manifestation of the same broader mapping of external selves onto internal selves, and the forces and barriers of our external world onto those of our internal world.

Let us set forth some similar analyses for the other modals' epistemic uses, attempting to apply our root-modal analyses from section 3.2 to the speaker's reasoning process rather than to the subject's action. We must now recast forces and barriers as premises in the mental world, since no other kinds of obstruction/force exist in that world. As we shall see, once that crucial mapping of forces and barriers onto premises has been done, the root- and epistemic-modal senses look more obviously parallel than without such a mapping. The majority of the root modals refer to various forces, which is reasonable, since we recognize many different varieties of force in the sociophysical world. In the epistemic domain, we have no contrast between internal forces (as in real-world *need*) and external forces (as in *have to*). Nor can we differentiate between kinds of authority or obligation; *should* and *ought* cannot refer to moral force (as opposed to authority or threats, for example) in a world where no morality exists. In all of the following examples, I shall contrast the use of a modal in its real-world sense (a) with its corresponding usage in the epistemic domain (b).

May (19a) John may go.
              "John is not barred by (my or some other) authority from going."
     (19b) John may be there.
              "I am not barred by my premises from the conclusion that he is there."
Must (20a) You must come home by ten. (Mom said so.)
              "The direct force (of Mom's authority) compels you to come home by ten."
     (20b) You must have been home last night.
              "The available (direct) evidence compels me to the conclusion that you were home."

This epistemic analysis of (20b) takes the premises in the speaker's mind as parallel to the force of authority in (20a). Note that the usual *reluctance* which is assumed to exist in the compelled person in (20a) has no counterpart in (20b). Such a contrast is a natural consequence of the differences between the sociophysical world and the epistemic world. In the real world, we don't usually use force unless we need to overcome reluctance on the part of the person we are forcing. But we do not view our mental processes as being affected by such reluctance, or by anything other than the available premises. Furthermore, in the real world, force is usually resented by the victim because freedom is valued. But in the world of reasoning, we wish to have our conclusions forced or restricted by premises (not by external sociophysical forces like threats) because this gives us more certainties within our belief system, and knowledge is valued.

Can (21a) I can lift fifty pounds.
"Some potentiality enables me to lift 50 lbs."
(21b) You can't have lifted fifty pounds.
"Some set of premises dis-enables me from concluding that you lifted 50 lbs."

Positive *can* is almost unusable in an epistemic sense.[17] But its negative and interrogative forms are quite acceptable (cf. "Can that be true?") and have the reading of questioned or negated epistemic enablement on the part of the speaker.

Ought to (22a) You ought to go.
"Certain forces (of moral obligation) influence you towards going."
(22b) That ought to be the right answer.
"The available set of premises (mental obligations or forces) influence me to conclude that that is the right answer."
Have to (23a) He has to be home by ten.
"Some force of authority compels him to be home by ten."
(23b) He has to be a New Yorker, with that accent.
"The available premises, including his accent, compel me to conclude he's from New York."
Need to (24a) He needs to go to the grocery store.
"Some internal forces (e.g. wanting to eat tonight) compel him to go to the store."
(24b) No, he needn't be a New Yorker – he could just have lived there a long time, or imitate accents well.
"The available premises do *not* force me to conclude that he's a New Yorker – they could also lead to other conclusions."

Once again, these analyses show the parallelism between root and epistemic uses of modals. Sociophysical forces acting on the subject are taken as analogous to the logical "force" of premises acting on the speaker's reasoning processes. Note that *need* (like *can*) is epistemic only in its negative and interrogative forms.

Will (*shall* is not epistemic)
(25a) John will come.
"The present state of affairs will proceed to the future event of John's arrival."
(25b) (hearing phone ring) That will be John.
"My present theory that that is John will proceed to future verification/confirmation."

Distal forms used epistemically (see the discussion of root distals, section 3.2).

These distal forms express past or conditional epistemic modalities.

Might (26a) He might go. (conditional)
"If some conditions were fulfilled, then my premises would not bar me from concluding that he will go."
(26b) I thought he might go. (past or conditional)
(The past (root) reading is simply the past of root *may*; the conditional (epistemic) reading is as above [26a])

Note that conditionals with no expressed *if*-clause often have conditions so general as to become simply dubitatives; but this is a general crosslinguistic fact about conditional forms.

Would (27) The folks you saw with John would be his parents. (conditional)
"If some conditions (like having full data) were fulfilled, my theory that they were his parents would proceed to future verification."
(28) When that phone rang, it would (certainly) be John. I was sure of it. (past)
(past tense of the epistemic *will* in [25a])
Could (29) That could be the right choice for the living-room curtains. (conditional)
"If some unspecified conditions were fulfilled, the available data would enable me to conclude that that's the right choice for the curtains."
(30) I was dumbfounded: it simply couldn't be true.
(past tense of epistemic *can* as in [21a])
Should (31) John should be easy to talk to.

As previously mentioned, *should* is an odd distal form. Perhaps because of its dissociation from its rare present form *shall*, it has become only minimally conditional (there is no contrast with a non-conditional form any more). The relevant condition appears to be something very general like "if all goes right" or "if all goes as expected." Thus the epistemic *should* in (31) is a barely conditional expression of epistemic obligation, verging on synonymy with *ought*. Since *shall* has no epistemic reading, it may only be by association with *ought* that *should* has developed such an interpretation.

Non-auxiliary (conjugated) modals like *have to, need to*, as previously mentioned, have past but no independent conditional forms. Their (regular) past-tense epistemic uses do not require discussion here.

The preceding description of epistemic modality has been nothing but a mapping of my proposed root-modal semantic analyses onto the epistemic domain. I do not propose that epistemic modals have complex generative-semantic predicate structures to differentiate them from their root counterparts. Rather, I propose that the root-modal meanings can be extended metaphorically from the "real" (sociophysical) world to the epistemic world. In the real world, the *must* in a sentence such as "John must go to all the department parties" is taken as indicating a *real-world force* imposed by the *speaker* (and/or by some other agent) which compels the *subject* of the sentence (or someone else) to *do the action* (or bring about its doing) expressed in the sentence. In the epistemic world the same sentence could be read as meaning "I must conclude that it is John's habit to go to the department parties (because I see his name on the sign-up sheet every time, and he's always out on those nights)." Here *must* is taken as indicating an *epistemic force* applied by some *body of premises* (the only thing that can apply epistemic force), which compels the *speaker* (or people in general) to reach the *conclusion* embodied in the sentence. This epistemic force is the counterpart, in the epistemic domain, of a forceful obligation in the sociophysical domain. The polysemy between root and epistemic senses is thus seen (as suggested above) as the conventionalization, for this group of lexical items, of a metaphorical mapping between domains.

Pragmatic factors will influence a hearer's interpretation of a particular uttered modal as operating in one domain or the other: for example, I swayed the interpretation of "John must go to all the department parties" toward an epistemic reading by adding a clause expressing a reason for reaching a conclusion. If, instead, I had added a clause expressing a real-world cause (such as "because he agreed to be bartender"), then the weight would have been towards a root reading. Sentences concerning past actions are strongly weighted towards an epistemic reading because real-world causality or modality can no longer influence frozen past events – I cannot seriously and cooperatively inform you that you are hereby put under an obligation, or given permission, to have done something yesterday. Conversely, modals in sentences concerning future actions are weighted towards a root reading, although an epistemic reading is not excluded. In other cases, the broader social context may disambiguate, rather than the immediate linguistic context. The fascinating fact is that the same (syntactic as well as lexical) form can naturally and regularly represent both of these different meanings. A polysemy analysis motivates this regularity.

Any sentence can be viewed under two aspects: as a description of a

[margin notes:] Modal: a force causes an action (speaker imposes force) epistemic: a force presses the speaker to make a conclusion of some sort future (default) root or real world / past epistemic

real-world situation or event, and as a self-contained part of our belief system (e.g. a conclusion or a premise). As descriptions, sentences describe real-world events and the causal forces leading up to those events; as *conclusions*, they are themselves understood as being the result of the epistemic forces which cause the train of reasoning leading to a conclusion. Modality is a specification of the force-dynamic environment of a sentence in either of these two worlds.

3.3.3   *Pragmatic interpretation of modal semantics in two worlds*
I suggested earlier in this chapter that although the root/epistemic contrast might profitably be viewed as polysemy, the difference between the imposing and describing uses of modals should be rather considered as a pragmatic generalization. If a modal verb simply expresses the application of some particular modality towards the event or action described in a sentence, pragmatic factors will determine what appropriate entity is understood as imposing the modality, and upon what entity it is imposed. Thus the root modals have a reading in which the speaker is taken as imposing the modality by stating it, and another reading in which some other entity (which may be elsewhere specified in the discourse) is the source of the modality. In saying "You must be home by ten," a parent could impose an obligation on a child, or an older sibling could report the obligation imposed by the parent. In saying "John can have three cookies," I could be granting permission or listing the maximum allowance given to him by his new diet. However, as stated in R. Lakoff (1972a), there is a tendency for the describer or reporter of modality to be taken as sympathetic to the imposer, especially with the monomorphemic modals such as *must* (as opposed to *have to*), but this is not obligatory.

The imposing/reporting contrast has interesting parallels with Searle's (1979) assertion/declaration distinction; like certain other (rather restricted) domains, modals are an area of language where speakers can either simply describe or actually mold by describing. Thus, for example, "You are now husband and wife" could be the words used to *create* the legal bond of marriage (if said by the right person in the right context), or it could be a description of the resulting married state. Unlike the imposition of an obligation or some other modality by the use of a modal verb, there is a complex legal and social structure surrounding marriage, and a specific institutional authority which enables a speaker to create a valid marriage by uttering certain words. One could, alternatively, emulate analyses (Austin 1962; Searle 1969, 1979, among others) of the dual uses of speech-act verbs, and say that modals can be used descriptively or *performatively*. Just as "I request a xerox copy of Grice's article" could either constitute the actual performance of a speech act of requesting, or (in a context such as "Whenever I teach that course…") a description of a request, so modals can create or describe modality. Interestingly, Searle (in press) has brought these two analyses together in the case of performative verbs; he now argues that all performative speech-acts are declarations – speech being an area where we have an inherent right to mold the world by speaking. This seems a very reasonable viewpoint to me, and could equally well apply to the modals, in those areas where we can impose modality on others.

There are areas of modality which cannot, by their very nature, be imposed by people on each other. These include what are sometimes called the *dynamic*[18] root-modal senses, referring to ability and disposition. Thus it is impossible for me to performatively create a modality of ability by saying "You can speak French," although I can performatively create a modality of social permission by saying "You can/may speak French," or a modality of obligation by saying "You must speak French."[19]

Thus, in interpretation of an utterance involving an English modal verb, the pragmatic factors involved in identifying the *source* or imposer of the modality include all our knowledge about the modality in question, and about the authority of contextually present agents (including prominently the speaker) to impose the relevant modality on the imposee(s).

Turning from the identity of the modality's imposer to the identity of the "target," the deep subject of the sentence is frequently taken as the modal imposee – the person carrying the obligation or receiving the permission expressed in root modals. This is natural, since obligations and permissions tend to be placed on the person viewed as responsible for doing the relevant action – often the agent, which in turn is often the subject in an active sentence. However, this interpretation of the subject of the clause as subject of the modality is only a pragmatic tendency (due to our general feelings about who is responsible) and *not* a fact about semantic structure. It has long been noted that a passive version of a modal sentence, although it has a different subject from the corresponding active sentence, may nonetheless be given the same modal interpretation: for example, both "Harry must wash the dishes" and "The dishes must be washed by Harry" impose an obligation on Harry. In fact, as R. Lakoff

(1972a) has pointed out, with a few pushes from the context we can see the imposed modality as being incumbent on almost *any* entity in (or outside of) the sentence. Modals are not simply "voice-neutral"; they are semantically neutral towards the choice of the imposee from among the sentence's NPs (or even from the context). Compare the following examples (from Lakoff):

(32) The witch must be kissed by every man in the room,
    ⎧ (a) or the leader of the coven will demote her to leprechaun. ⎫
    ⎨ (b) or they'll all be turned into star-nosed moles. ⎬
    ⎩ (c) because that's the law. ⎭

In (a) the obligation to get kissed rests primarily with the witch; in (b) the men are the ones responsible; and in (c) the obligation rests on all the participants, or even on the world at large. Another possible interpretation of the first clause of (32) in isolation would be that the hearer is to see to it that the kissing occurs – hence the obligation would devolve on the hearer. In short, any pragmatically reasonable interpretation of the identities of the modal imposer and imposee is possible. Pragmatically unreasonable interpretations, such as the identification of hearer with modality imposer, or identification of some non-volitional agent with the modality imposee (for example, imposing on the dishes the responsibility to get washed) would take a great deal of context, if indeed they are possible at all.

For epistemic modality, the story is simpler than for root modality. In the epistemic world, only premises count as forces or barriers. The only kind of event is a logical conclusion (or the verification of a theory); and it even has to be the speaker's own conclusion, because the force-dynamic structure of other people's reasoning processes is not readily accessible to us. Sometimes there seems to be a feeling that our reasoning process is a rather general one, which our interlocutor may share – but the speaker's own reasoning process is always the primary subject of epistemic modality.[20]

Pragmatic factors explain why modals can be used either to impose or to describe real-world modality, while only description of epistemic modalities is possible. Sociophysical modalities can be imposed by speakers – epistemic obligations and forces cannot be imposed by anything but premises. Thus a performative use of sociophysical modality (doing by describing) is natural, while it is impossible for the epistemic modalities. Epistemic-modal sentences thus lack the multiple ambiguities inherent in the pragmatic interpretation of real-world modality: there is no possible doubt as to the nature of the mental modality's imposer and imposee.

This section has presented an analysis of epistemic modality not as a kind of modality unrelated to root modality, but as an essentially metaphorical application of our sociophysical modal concepts to the epistemic world. We have seen that such a unified viewpoint is possible if we analyze modality in terms of general forces and barriers – evidently these are the basic sociophysical concepts in terms of which we understand our mental processes. In fact, I have argued that with the proper appeal to our pragmatic interpretation processes, there is no need to differentiate many aspects of the semantic structure of root and epistemic modals; in particular, there is no need to assume that there is a semantic specification of modality-imposers and imposees built into the meanings of the two kinds of modals. I have, nonetheless, also argued for keeping the two senses distinct, with a metaphorical mapping linking the two domains in regular, and (given the broader metaphorical system of the language) perhaps even predictable, ways. This metaphorical mapping preserves the directional relationship between the two domains.

I have elsewhere (Sweetser 1986) given reasons why I think the root/epistemic contrast is not best treated as two purely pragmatically conditioned interpretations of a single semantics, but rather as a motivated polysemy relationship. One reason is that the metaphorical mapping involved appears to be a linguistic convention: it is a fact about the semantics of English that these specific lexical items bear both these related senses. It is likewise true that such a polysemy is crosslinguistically common. But it is not the case (as we might expect if the modals were simply monosemous) that all root modals must/can have epistemic uses – this is neither historically true for the English modals nor a crosslinguistic universal.

The following sections will further motivate the application of real-world modalities to the epistemic domain, by showing that those modalities are also extended to the domain of speech acts, and that not just modality, but causality in general, has extended uses in the epistemic and speech-act domains.

3.4   Speech-act verbs and speech-act modality

I have argued that our reason for applying the same modal verbs to the real world and to the epistemic world is that we view the epistemic world as having a force-dynamic structure parallel to that of the real world (allowing for differences in the actual *nature* of the forces and barriers involved). If this is so, then one might expect other parts of the English lexicon to manifest a similar tendency towards ambiguity between real-world force and epistemic force. And indeed several classes of lexical items (to be discussed in the two following chapters) can be applied to causal forces equally in both worlds. Although all of these classes have been recognized as ambiguous, so far as I know they have not previously been analyzed as parallel to the modal case. However, Tregidgo (1982) mentions the likelihood that the two readings of verbs such as *insist*, as exemplified in the (a) and (b) examples below, are a manifestation of a larger contrast between root and epistemic senses.

(33a) I insist { that you go to London.
on your going to London. }
(33b) I insist that you *did* go to London (though you may deny it).
(34a) I suggest that you leave the room now.
(34b) I suggest that you left the room to avoid being seen.
(35a) I expect him to be there. (ambiguous)
(35b) I expect that he's there.

In each of the (a) sentences, the speech act involves the speaker's interaction in the force-dynamics of a real-world situation – the insistence or suggestion is on some actual real-world result to be produced. In the (b) sentences, on the other hand, the same sorts of speech-act interactions are directed at the *epistemic* structure: insistence or suggestion that a proposition be believed or accepted as true, or expectation that it will prove to be true. As Tregidgo says, even the verb *agree* is ambiguous between agreement *to* (do something) and agreement *that* (something is true). Given the understanding that any sentence can be treated as an expression of some state of affairs in the real world, or as a conclusion in our world of reasoning, it is reasonable that a verb such as *insist* should be used to express insistence on either the real-world *doing* of the action expressed in its clausal complement, or the epistemic *concluding* of the truth of the proposition constituted by that complement.

It is interesting to note that there is slightly more formal marking of the distinction between root and epistemic readings of speech-act verbs than between the different readings of the modals; although *I expect him to be there* may be ambiguous just like *He ought to be there*, we formally distinguish *I insist that he be there* from *I insist that he is/was there*.

Such verbs as *insist* are, then, not merely an argument for forces (such as insistence) being mappable from the real world (the content world) to the epistemic domain, but also for our viewing all linguistic expression as existing in these two domains simultaneously. Any actual utterance, however, is more than an epistemic reaction to a proposition about some content; it is a *speech act* achieved *by means of* the expression of that proposition about that content. One might therefore possibly expect some reflection of the speech act's own internal force-dynamic structure in the use of modal verbs and similarly ambiguous lexical items. And indeed we find such a reflection. Modal-verb uses such as those in (36) and (37) do not appear to fit into the standard root/epistemic dichotomy:

(36) He may be a university professor, but he sure is dumb.[21]
(37) There may be a six-pack in the fridge, but we have work to do.

The relevant reading of (36) and (37) is the reading which presupposes the truth of each example's first clause. Under this reading, (36) means something like "I admit that he's a university professor, and I nonetheless insist that he's dumb," where *I admit* has been used to roughly gloss *may* and *I nonetheless insist* to gloss *but*.[22] Example (37), in a context where the interlocutor has offered refreshments by saying "There's a six-pack in the fridge," means something like "I acknowledge your offer, and I nonetheless refuse it." These readings are to be contrasted with the readings of (38) and (39), where the modal *may* has a normal epistemic sense:

(38) He may be a university professor, but I doubt it because he's so dumb.
(39) There may be a six-pack in the fridge, but I'm not sure because Joe had friends over last night.

Appropriate paraphrases of the *may* in the first clauses of (38) and (39) might be something like "It is *possible* that..." or "I am not barred from concluding that..." But how does the root (absent-barrier) sense of *may* apply in (36) and (37)?

I propose that (36) and (37) may be paraphrased as (36') and (37'):

(36') I *do not bar* from our (joint) conversational world *the statement* that he is a university professor, but...
(37') I *do not bar* from our conversational world *your offer* of beer, but...

Notice the ease with which we could also paraphrase (36) by "I'll *allow* (that/as how) he's a professor, but..." Verbs such as *admit* and *allow* (meaning *not bar from*) normally can't be used to mean admission of an interlocutor's non-assertive speech acts (hence these glosses needed to be replaced with *acknowledge* in paraphrasing [37]). Legal language might be adduced as evidence of possible broader uses of *admit/allow*, however, as in "We can't *admit* that statement as evidence" or "I must (*dis*)*allow* Mr Jones' plea."

In (36) and (37), then, *may* does not indicate the absence of a real (content)-world barrier, nor of an epistemic barrier, but rather the absence of a barrier in the *conversational* world. The interlocutor is being *allowed* by the speaker to treat a certain statement as appropriate or reasonable, or to present an offer. If "allowing" sounds a little grudging (normally we don't think of permission for speech acts such as statements), it should be noted that (36) and (37) do display a certain grudging spirit on the part of the speaker. In each case the use of *may* seems to be saying "I'll allow *this* much, but nothing further" – i.e. the speaker's "admission" of the first conjunct is not to be taken as indicating that the speaker agrees that professors are all smart in (36), or that the speaker *accepts* the acknowledged offer in (37).[23]

If my analysis is correct, then modality applies not only to the content and epistemic domains but also to the conversational interaction itself – a domain which is inherently present to be referred to in any speech interaction, just as the content and epistemic domains are present.[24] It is difficult to find examples parallel to (36) and (37) using other modal verbs besides *may*; but there are other possible applications of modal verbs at the conversational level, which seem to include all of the other modals quite regularly. Consider (40)–(43):[25]

(40) Mondale advisor giving directions to speech writer:
   "Reagan *will/must* be a nice guy (as far as the content of the speech is concerned), even if we criticize his policies."
(41) Editor to journalist:
   "OK, Peking *can* be Beijing; but you can't use 'Praha' for Prague."
(42) To smoker of long cigarette, from speaker who recognizes that "cigar" dialectally signifies "long cigarette":
   "In New Orleans, you *would* be smoking a cigar right now."
(43) Lawyer to plaintiff:
   "Remember, the mobsters *can* be as guilty as you like, but you mustn't suggest the police are implicated, or the jury will stop being sympathetic."

The second clauses of (41) and (43) suggest appropriate glosses for the modals in the first clauses:

(41') OK, *you can refer to* Peking as Beijing...
(43') Remember, *you can say that* the mobsters are as guilty as you like...

Similar paraphrases work for (40) and (42):

(40') The speech *will/must talk about* Reagan as if he were a nice guy...

(42') In New Orleans, *one would* $\left\{ \begin{array}{l} \textit{say } \text{that you're smoking a cigar.} \\ \textit{call } \text{what you are smoking a cigar.} \end{array} \right\}$

In all of these examples, the modality clearly applies to some speech act in question; in no sense is epistemic possibility/necessity or real-world permission/obligation being predicated of the *contents* of these sentences. For example, (40) cannot be understood (under the relevant reading) as being about Reagan's future as a nice guy, or Reagan's being obligated to behave nicely, or the speaker's certainty about Reagan's niceness.

In some cases (notably [41] and [42]) a use/mention distinction seems to be involved, in that the speaker is applying the relevant modality to the choice of linguistic *form*, not to the content. But cases like (43) show fairly clearly that this use of modality is not restricted to issues of form – in (43) it is the *purport* of the plaintiff's future statement that is in question. These are all cases of modals being applied to the speech-act world; whether they apply to the production of a given form or to the production of a given content seems not to matter.[26]

It is not clear whether (36) and (37) should be grouped with (40)–(43) or not. The presupposition of the first clause's truth in (36) and (37) seems to show different behavior on the part of *may* in those clauses. On the other hand, *may* does not seem to be as freely usable as the other modals in sentences like (40)–(43); although it might be possible to use it in (43), it seems marginal, and I find it anomalous in (40), where one might expect it to be good (*can* is fine in [40]). It may be that speech-act *may* has been specialized to the sort of use exemplified in (36) and (37).

Speech-act-domain uses of modal verbs (or *metalinguistic* uses, as we would probably call them in examples [40]–[43] at least) need a good deal more investigation. However, it seems evident that a modal verb may be interpreted as applying the relevant modality to:

1.   the content of the sentence: the real-world event *must* or *may* take place;

2.   the epistemic entity represented by the sentence: the speaker is forced
        to, or (not) barred from, *concluding* the truth of the sentence;
3.   the speech act represented by the sentence: the speaker (or people in
        general) is forced to, or (not) barred from, *saying* what the sentence
        says.

It is worth commenting on the fact that modals can be used either to
impose or to *describe* (report) modality in both the content and speech-act
domains, but can only describe in the epistemic domain (see section 3.3,
above). The speech-act domain is, like the general "real-world" content
domain, an area wherein speakers can suppose themselves able to mold as
well as to describe.

It is not clear why speech-act uses of modals have the (relatively
restricted) readings that they do; for example, they generally do *not* refer
to the speech act being performed by the speaker. In order to apply a
modality to the speech act being performed, one would typically say, e.g.,

(44) I *must tell* you that your father wants you home, though I'd rather not.

However, it is rare to express certain modalities towards the speech act
being performed; although not rare to *request* permission, it is rare to
assert it:

(45) *May* I ask you where you are going?
(46) *?I *may* ask you where you are going.

And if there is a general obstacle to many possible uses of *may* reflexively
referring to the current speech-act, then why should the lexicalized use of
may standing alone in this sense be possible? So the question of
interpretation of speech-act modals may depend at least partly on general
principles of expression of modality towards speech acts, whether the
speech acts are implicitly or explicitly performed.

3.5   Conclusions

This chapter has set forth an analysis of linguistic modality as being
generalized or extended from the real-world domain to the domains of
reasoning and speech acts. The advantage of such an approach is that it
allows us to unify our account of the contrast between root and epistemic
senses of the modal verbs, and of other similarly ambiguous lexical items
such as *insist*. Such words are ambiguous in a systematic and regular
manner between root, epistemic, and (if applicable) speech-act senses, and

the epistemic and speech-act senses are extensions of the root senses. My proposed analysis is also coherent with the historical and developmental linguistic evidence, which suggests that an extension from the socio-physical domain to the epistemic domain would be normal, while an extension in the opposite direction would be unnatural.

Talmy's approach to deontic modality and causality in terms of forces and barriers has given us a way to look at root-modal senses which can be extended to the epistemic and speech-act domains. Attempts to find single superordinate analyses which include both root- and epistemic-modal meanings have proven unsuccessful (see Ehrman 1966), and would be even less helpful if applied to speech-act uses of modal verbs as well. But the problem is removed by taking into account our understanding of mental processes (and of the current speech-act utterance) as involving forces and barriers analogous to those involved in "real-world" physical and social interactions. Without taking into account this background metaphor, trying to unify deontic- and epistemic-modal meaning is like trying to find the common semantic features of "optimism" and "pink sunglasses" without basing our analysis on the knowledge that physical sight is a primary metaphor for world-*view* in the mental domain. But given the priority of the real world, and the structuring of the epistemic and speech-act worlds in terms of that prior world, it then follows naturally that the root understanding of modality will be readily extended to apply in all three worlds.

Among current semantic theories, Fauconnier's (1985) concept of "mental spaces" is particularly useful for an understanding of these multi-domain ambiguities. Fauconnier would say that the three domains I have discussed (content, epistemic, and speech act) are three mental spaces, and that certainty is the *counterpart* in the epistemic domain of compulsion in the real-world domain, while epistemic possibility is the counterpart of root possibility or permission.[27] Polysemy structures (like Fauconnier's reference structures) seem to be able to name counterparts in different domains with the same lexical item.

The basic semantic analysis of the modals which I have proposed is a very simple one. It would not extend so easily into the epistemic domain if it explicitly mentioned a complex set of possible identities for real-world imposers and targets (imposees) of modalities. Rather, it leaves these identities to pragmatic interpretation. I consider this to be a further advantage of my analysis, since the semantics of the modals appears to be indeterminate in this area. That is, the semantic structure of the modal verbs does not explicitly pick out either subject or object (or any specific syntactic or semantic role) as the participant on whom the modality rests; rather it is the pragmatic factors inherent in the speech-act setting, together with our understanding of utterances as multi-leveled objects, which easily account for the possible ambiguities of modals with respect to the origins and targets of forces.

An utterance is content, epistemic object, and speech act all at once. There are areas of meaning which are naturally circumscribed within one of the three worlds in which utterances exist. But our linguistic treatment of causal force, and of the closely allied concepts of different modal forces, can be more fully understood by examining linguistic treatment of counterparts in more than one of the three domains.

4 Conjunction, coordination, and subordination

While modality may offer self-evident cases of polysemy (between the root and epistemic senses), there are other areas of the lexicon where few would even suggest that differences in usage correspond to a polysemy between linguistic domains. The purpose of this chapter is to show that conjunctions, like modal verbs, are "ambiguous" among usages in the content, epistemic, and conversational domains. A simple analysis of conjunctions as logical operators will prove far too weak to explain the ambiguities in their usage, or to account for the fact that ambiguities between domains are to be observed equally in simple conjunction (and disjunction) and complex lexical conjunctions such as *therefore* or *although*. Not only must conjunctions be given a more complex lexical-semantic analysis, but their contribution to sentence semantics must be analyzed in the context of an utterance's polyfunctional status as a bearer of content, as a logical entity, and as the instrument of a speech act.

I will give arguments suggesting that (at least for some conjunctions) a lexical-polysemy analysis is implausible, and that instead these conjunctions are examples of what Horn (1985) has called *pragmatic ambiguity*. In polysemy, a morpheme has several related semantic values; in pragmatic ambiguity (see chapter 1), a single semantics is pragmatically applied in different ways according to pragmatic context. It is interesting to observe that our three-way understanding of utterances as content, epistemic entity, and speech act is relevant to this pragmatic-ambiguity structure, as well as to the polysemy structure of lexical items such as the modals.

4.1 Causal and adversative conjunctions[1]

4.1.1 Three readings of causal and adversative conjunction
Let us begin by comparing the uses of *because* in the sentences below:

(1a) John came back because he loved her.
(1b) John loved her, because he came back. *causality cannot be reversed*
(1c) What are you doing tonight, because there's a good movie on.

In the first example, (1a), real-world causality connects the two clauses: that is to say, his love was the real-world cause of his coming back. In the *uses* second sentence, however, the causality would appear to be reversed, but *of because* is not. Example (1b) does *not* most naturally mean that the return caused the love in the real world; in fact, under the most reasonable interpretation, the real-world causal connection could still be the one stated in (1a), though not necessarily. Rather, (1b) is normally understood as meaning that the speaker's *knowledge* of John's return (as a premise) causes the *conclusion* that John loved her.[2]

Going a step further, (1c) would be a totally incomprehensible sentence if the conjunction were understood in the content domain. Since the main clause is not even a statement, the *because*-clause cannot be understood as stating the real-world cause of the event or situation described in the main clause. Rather, the *because*-clause gives the cause of the *speech act* embodied by the main clause. The reading is something like "I *ask* what you are doing tonight because I want to suggest that we go see this good movie." The "causality" (or more correctly, *enablement*, since we are to take the statement as justifying and hence enabling the question) is Gricean or Searlean. In order for a suggestion to be felicitous, I must first know that compliance is not already impossible beforehand; hence, conversely, I can justify an inquiry as to possibility on the grounds that I hope to follow it up with a suggestion (see Searle 1969; Gordon and Lakoff 1971).

As with modals, there are examples where only context can disambiguate the domain of conjunction, e.g. (2):

(2) She went, because she left her book in the movie theater last night.

It would be possible to read (2) either as an assertion of a person's departure, followed by a real-world reason for the departure (intention to recover the lost book), or as a logical conclusion: I know she went (to the movies), because I discovered that she left her book in the movie theater. (The commaless reading pretty much forces a content-conjunction rather than an epistemic-conjunction interpretation, but I will discuss this phenomenon later on.) Given sufficient context, we can almost always force either a content-conjunction reading or an epistemic-conjunction reading on any pair of clauses conjoined with *because*; it is just harder to find reasonable contexts for some readings than for others. Thus, for example, (1a) above could be taken (with a comma added) as meaning that I *conclude* that he must have come back, because I *know* that he loved her; while (1b) could be taken as meaning that his return actually caused his love in some way. The exception to this rule, of course, is speech-act conjunction; if an utterance is imperative or interrogative in form, then it cannot reasonably be causally conjoined to another utterance except at the speech-act level.[3]

My point, then, is that conjunction may be interpreted as applying in one of (at least) three domains; and that the choice of a "correct" interpretation depends not on form, but on a pragmatically motivated choice between viewing the conjoined clauses as representing content units, logical entities, or speech acts.

Application in three different domains is easily exemplified for the whole range of causal and adversative conjunctions: the ambiguities are perhaps the clearest for this class of conjunction, although (as we will see) they are present in the usage of a much larger class of lexical items. Thus *therefore, since, so, although*, and *despite*[4] (properly a preposition, forming part of a frequently used conjoining phrase *despite the fact that*) all show such multiple usage. The (a) examples below are cases of content conjunction; the (b) examples are epistemic conjunction; and the (c) examples are speech-act conjunction:

(3a) *Since* John wasn't there, we decided to leave a note for him.
      (His absence caused our decision in the real world.)
(3b) *Since* John isn't here, he has (evidently) gone home.
      (The *knowledge* of his absence causes my *conclusion* that he has gone home.)
(3c) *Since* $\left\{ \begin{array}{l} \text{we're on the subject,} \\ \text{you're so smart,} \end{array} \right\}$ when was George Washington born?

      (I *ask* you because we're on the subject, or because you're so smart – the fact that we're on the subject, for example, enables my *act* of asking the question.)
(4a) The rules cannot be broken, *therefore* you will have to spend two hours collecting trash.
      (The rules' unbreakability causes your fate in the real world.)
(4b) The rules cannot be broken, *therefore* the Dean knew some way around them that allowed him to hire John.
      (My *knowledge* of the rules' unbreakability causes my *conclusion* that the Dean knew a way around them.)

(4c) The rules cannot be broken, *therefore* "No."
      (The rules' unbreakability causes my *act of saying* "No.")

(5a) He heard me calling, *so* he came.
      (The hearing caused the coming, in the real world.)

(5b) (You say he's deaf, but) he came, *so* he heard me calling.
      (The knowledge of his arrival causes the *conclusion* that he heard me calling.)

(5c) Here we are in Paris, *so* what would you like to do on our first evening here?
      (Our presence in Paris enables my *act of asking* what you would like to do.)

(6a) *Although* he $\begin{Bmatrix} \text{didn't hear me calling,} \\ \text{could hardly walk,} \end{Bmatrix}$ he came and and saved my life.

      (His coming occurred in spite of his $\begin{Bmatrix} \text{not hearing,} \\ \text{inability to walk,} \end{Bmatrix}$

      which might naturally have led to his not coming.

(6b) *Although* he came and saved me, he hadn't heard me calling for help. (The *fact* that he didn't hear me is true in spite of the *fact* that he came, which might reasonably have led me to *conclude* that he had heard.)

(6c) *Although* I sympathize with your problems, get the paper in tomorrow!
      (I *command* you, in spite of my sympathy.)

(7a) *Despite* their threats, she kept right on doing her job.
      (The real-world *doing* occurred despite the threats.)

(7b) *Despite* the fact that she never wavered, (we now know that) she was being threatened the whole time.
      (The *knowledge* of the threats occurs despite the likelihood of the contrary conclusion.)

(7c) *Despite* all the regulations about TA-student relationships, how about dinner at Chez Panisse tonight?
      (The *speech act* of inviting occurs despite the apparent obstacles.)

Note that the statements, as well as other kinds of speech acts, are subject to causal conjunction. The stated cause then naturally relates to the conditions of making the assertion in question:

(8) The answer's on page 200, *since* you'll never find it for yourself.
     (I make this assertion *because* it gives you information which you can't acquire independently. A Gricean condition of informativeness is thus invoked as the "cause" of a statement.)

(9) Mary loves you very much, Tom – *although* I'm sure you already know that.
     (I make this assertion *despite* its lack of Gricean informativeness, a violation which I feel bound to comment upon.)

Because (as I have tried to make clear) the choice of domain for the interpretation of conjunction is essentially a pragmatic one, certain contents almost force interpretation at a given level. Thus, for example, (8) and (9) are extremely difficult to interpret as examples of anything but speech-act conjunction: the answer's actually being on page 200, and my belief that it is on page 200, are equally independent of my interlocutor's ability to locate it there. An example like (7b), with explicit mention of the speaker's knowledge state, practically forces an epistemic interpretation, as does (10):

(10) *Since* you are wearing your new tennis shorts, you aren't going to the library, I conclude/guess/suppose.

It is harder to force a content-conjunction reading, since almost anything which can cause or impede events in the real world can also cause (or impede) our conclusions about these events (although the converse is not the case). However, we have briefly mentioned the fact that the commaless examples (e.g. [1a]) require a content reading, and I will discuss this in more detail below.

I have tried to show clearly the three possible usages of words such as *because* – a task which is the more necessary because such ambiguities have been treated incompletely elsewhere. Ross (1970) and Davison (1973) both treat examples of what I call "epistemic conjunction" as cases of speech-act conjunction – i.e., they interpret sentences like (11) as meaning something like "I *say* to you that he loves me because I am justified by the evidence to that effect":

(11) He loves me, *because* he wouldn't have proofread my thesis if he didn't.

What I trust has been clarified by the arguments above is the impossibility of following Ross' proposal. There is a class of causal-conjunction uses in which the causality is that between premise and conclusion in the speaker's mind (as in [11]), and there is another class of uses in which the causality actually involves the speech act itself (as in [8] and [9] or the [c] examples above). Note that (11) could perfectly well be used to represent a thought sequence pure and simple; following our omniscient narrator into our heroine's mind, we might find her thinking (11) without any speech act at all. The *because*-clause may in fact secondarily buttress a speech act of assertion (once again assuming [11] to be a speech act), inasmuch as our conversational rules make it incumbent upon us to say things we believe to be true, rather than things we understand to be false. But its primary function, surely, is to explain the epistemic act of drawing the conclusion "He loves me." The *because*-clause is fully sufficient as a cause for the act of concluding, but evidence of truth need not by any means be a sufficient cause for the act of stating something. Speech-act conjunction examples, as we have seen, would more likely refer to the *relevance* or *irrelevance* of a state of affairs as causing or impeding the speaker's action. Other possible causal explanations for, or impediments to, an act of stating include the hearer's probable ability or willingness to respond appropriately (for example, to respond by believing a statement, answering a question, fulfilling a request, or obeying a command). Thus examples of speech-act conjunction like (12) and (13) occur:

(12) I'm innocent, *although* I know you won't believe me. *speech-act*
     (I *assert* this despite the fact that you are not an appropriately receptive hearer.)
(13) It may seem crazy to most people, but *since* you say you've had similar experiences yourself – I saw my father's ghost on the battlements last night.
     (I only *assert* this because you are an appropriate hearer.)

Once again, note the impossibility of a content-conjunction reading of such examples. Even though the form of (12) may be precisely parallel to that of examples like (6a), the reading of the conjunction cannot be parallel; there is no way in which we can reasonably interpret a person's guilt or innocence as dependent on whether their story is believed by a hearer, whereas we easily and normally understand *assertion* of guilt or innocence to be influenced by a hearer's cynicism or credulity.

Causal conjunction in the speech-act domain, then, indicates causal *cause* explanation of the speech act being performed, while in the epistemic *not expressly* domain a causal conjunction will mark the cause of a belief or a *stated in* conclusion, and in the content domain it will mark "real-world" causality *the speech-* of an event. All of this seems only too natural, given the existence and *act* nature of the three domains. But that in turn brings us back to the question of justifying my claims as to the existence of the domains. The first major argument is one which I have already advanced in the preceding discussion of modality, and which I will continue to use in succeeding discussions of similar issues in other lexical fields of English: why should ambiguities of this sort recur so frequently? If we failed to notice our general application of "content-domain" vocabulary (such as the root modals) to the epistemic domain, we would have no explanation for any of the large number of lexical items which show regular, parallel ambiguities of this kind. That is to say, postulating the existence of these different domains as part of the background to semantics is useful, in that it allows us to state generalizations which we would otherwise miss.

The second argument is that the three domains to which I refer exist, independent of the polysemous vocabulary under analysis; by which I mean simply that it seems *reasonable* to talk about utterances as having content, speech-act force, and some kind of epistemic status. Such distinctions are useful for other, more general explanatory purposes. We are not multiplying domains without necessity; indeed, we would be surprised if extra domains kept *randomly* surfacing to cause ambiguity in our language. Rather we are using known facts about the multi-faceted nature of language to explain lexical ambiguity.

My final argument for the existence of these domains is that there are languages whose vocabularies distinguish more clearly among the domains than is the case in English. Although Eng. *because* is triply polysemous, we may note that *since* already has a strong tendency towards an epistemic or a speech-act reading, rather than towards a content-conjunction reading. But Fr. *parce que* "because" is used specifically for content conjunction, while *puisque* is the correct causal conjunction at the epistemic or speech-act level.[5] This shows that English did not *have* to use the same vocabulary for real-world causation and epistemic causation. We should note that this makes the English polysemy case a more interesting one than it would otherwise be: we have concrete proof that the domains in question are distinct and distinguishable, and yet we can see that there are too many systematic polysemies of this variety for the domains to be unrelated. The relationship thus cries out for explanation; and that explanation is impossible except in the larger context of our general linguistic understanding of thought and speech.

4.1.2 *Comma intonation and causal conjunction*

If my analysis is correct, we might suppose it likely that differences in usage between, e.g., content-domain conjunction and epistemic-domain conjunction might turn out to be explicable in terms of the difference between the two domains, just as certain differences between root and epistemic modality fall out from the differences between the domains. One obvious question which I have not yet addressed is why, for those causal and adversative conjunctions which do not require a comma separating the clauses, the commaless conjunction cases are obligatorily interpreted as cases of content conjunction. And I now propose that this apparent quirk of usage is a result of the inherent and independently motivated differences between the content domain and the epistemic and speech-act domains.

Chafe (1984) notes that "bound" (commaless) *because*-clauses have a readily accessible reading which *presupposes* the truth of the main clause, and *asserts* only the causal relation between the clauses. Thus (14) may be read as presupposing that Anna loves Victor, and asserting simply that this love is caused by her memories of her first love:

knowledge it

(14) Anna loves Victor *because* he reminds her of her first love. *presupposed*

On the other hand, (15)'s comma intonation at the end of the main clause forces the alternative reading, wherein Anna's love for Victor is asserted, and the cause is asserted, too. (This is assuming we *don't* give [15] an epistemic-conjunction reading, which would take it as asserting both my *conclusion* that Anna loves Victor and the causal relation between that conclusion and the relevant data.)

(15) Anna loves Victor, because he reminds her of her first love. *As two separate assertions*

   The comma in (15) appears to mark a phrase-final intonation drop at the end of the sentence-initial main clause, rather than simply marking a pause. This clause-final intonation drop, then, marks the presentation of a clause as an independent assertion rather than as a presupposition. In content-conjunction cases such as (14) and (15), either possibility exists: i.e. a speaker could equally well have a reason for saying (14) and presupposing that Anna loves Victor, or for saying (15) and asserting it. The option is not, however, present with all conjunctions: in fact, most causal and adversative conjunctions require comma intonation and assertion of both conjuncts, as in (16) and (17) (assuming we can get a content-conjunction reading for [16]):

commalest — content domain

(16) Anna loves Victor, *since* he reminds her of her first love.
(17) Anna loves Victor, *although* he doesn't resemble her first love.

The commaless equivalents of (16) and (17) are not very plausible sentences, if they are possible at all (we have already commented above that *since* preferentially takes an epistemic or a speech-act reading – and we will see below that this may affect its occurrence in a commaless context). But for certain conjunctions, such as *because* and *despite*, both options exist.

   For epistemic-domain and speech-act-domain causal conjunction, however, a commaless intonation-pattern is impossible. Why should this be so? Commaless intonation tends to present an initial main clause as presupposed; and in content-conjunction cases the main clause has, as it were, the option of being treated as presupposed. But in epistemic causal-conjunction cases, the main clause represents the speaker's logical conclusion; and in speech-act causal-conjunction cases, the main clause represents the speech act being performed by the current utterance. Can either of these things reasonably be taken as presupposed material? Let's look at example (18):

(18) Anna loves Victor, *because* she told me so herself, and besides, she'd never have proofread his thesis otherwise.
(I conclude that she loves him *because* I know the relevant data.)

The speaker's internal act ("concluding that X") is precisely what must be asserted in example (18); or at any rate it is precisely what cannot be taken as presupposed (it is surely impossible to talk about *asserting* such an epistemic force, or the force of the current speech-act, in the way that one asserts the content of an assertive speech-act). Because the act of concluding is speaker-internal, it cannot be assumed as common knowledge between the speaker and the hearer, and hence cannot be presupposed. The speech act being performed is likewise something which cannot reasonably be taken as background already shared with the hearer: if it were really shared, the speech act would already have been performed.

It is harder to find examples of "potentially commaless" speech-act causal conjunction – i.e., cases where (a) the main clause precedes a subordinate clause which expresses causation or adversativity; (b) the "main clause" does not have some formal characteristic affecting its intonation (e.g., interrogative or imperative form); and (c) the relevant conjunction also *allows* commaless intonation in those cases. But something like (19) may be an example:

(19) No (you may not), because I can't take the responsibility for letting you do that.

Precisely the non-presupposable part of (19) is the speech act itself ("I say 'No'"), rather than the causal subordinate clause or even the auxiliary assertion of the causal relationship between the two clauses.

We may note here that there does exist a well-known class of cases where the force of the in-progress speech-act is *literally* asserted – namely, performative speech-acts. Thus it would be possible to rephrase (19) as the performative equivalent (19a):

(19a) *I tell you* no, because I can't take the responsibility for letting you do that.

Example (19a) performs the act of telling the hearer something *by* asserting that the act in question is being performed. Such cases confirm our earlier hypothesis that the current speech-act force cannot be presupposed;[6] the speech act is only performed by virtue of the actively assertive status of the performative clause. Compare (19a) and (19b), an apparent parallel with commaless intonation:

(19b) I tell you no because I can't take the responsibility for letting you do that (and not because I want to be mean).

Example (19b) can indeed be read as presupposing the act of telling – but, crucially, it *cannot* be read as performing it. My only reading of (19b) is one where the speaker is understood to have *already* told the hearer "no" (or habitually does so under certain circumstances), and is now just *explaining* this already-completed speech act by asserting a causal relation between some situation and the completed act. Example (19a), on the other hand, is ambiguous (like most performative utterances) between a performative interpretation equivalent to (19) and a straight descriptive interpretation like (19b) (though without the same presupposition of the main clause). My claim is that this ambiguity is possible only because of the comma intonation which indicates that the act of telling is asserted; and that this is why (19) has no possible commaless equivalent.

The same distinction can be observed in the epistemic domain: (20) is equivalent to only one of the two readings of (20a), and (20b) is equivalent only to the other reading of (20a):

(20) You're going to the library, because (I know) you wouldn't be taking your pack of books to the movies.
(20a) I conclude that you're going to the library, because I know you wouldn't be taking your pack of books to the movies.
(20b) I conclude that you're going to the library because I know you wouldn't be taking your pack of books to the movies.

Example (20) has only a reading wherein the act of concluding is expressed as concurrent with the speech act, while (20b) has only a reading wherein the act of concluding is presupposed and its cause is asserted. Example (20a) is ambiguous between a reading equivalent to (20) (but with the act of concluding overtly asserted rather than conveyed by the pragmatics) and a simple descriptive reading more closely equivalent to (20b) (although, once more, without the presupposition of the initial clause). The first reading might be called an epistemic performative reading – "I hereby conclude (or decide)," rather than "I hereby state (or ask or order)," as in performative speech-acts. An epistemic performative is interpreted essentially as an act of thinking out loud, rather than an act of describing one's thought processes subsequently. It is not the same as a performative speech-act, but an epistemic performative reading bears the same kind of relation to the equivalent descriptive reading that a performative speech-act bears to *its* corresponding descriptive reading: in the one case, the speaker is *doing* in saying, and in the other case the speaker is describing a separately performed action. But in order to "do in saying," the action described cannot already be part of a presupposed background. Hence (20) cannot (as an example of epistemic conjunction) have the commaless presupposition-bearing intonation; and (20b) (without commas), conversely, cannot have an epistemic-conjunction reading.

What emerges from the preceding discussion is the understanding that an essentially unitary semantic entity (such as *because*) (a) can not only be "ambiguous" by dint of being applicable to different domains; but (b) can even have different grammatical behavior when applied to these different domains – without necessarily being thereby several separate entities. Such regular contrasts in grammatical behavior, observed in large numbers of lexical items, may be due to our understanding of the relevant domains themselves, rather than to polysemy on the part of the lexical items in question.

We will now leave the area of causal/adversative conjunction, and continue to the larger area of conjunction in general. A discussion of *and, but,* and *or* (the most basic coordinating conjunctions of English) will show us that ambiguity between domains is not a property of causal and adversative conjunction alone.

4.2   *And, or,* and *but*

From the above discussions of modality and causal conjunction, it should be clear that our vocabulary of real-world force and causation is the basis for our lexicon of the epistemic and speech-act analogues of force and causation. The basic link-up is not (for example) between the content-domain usage of *because* and the epistemic-domain usage of *because*; rather, it is a more general link-up between real-world causality and the epistemic causation of a conclusion by premises. But we have seen, in chapter 2, the extent to which the *general* vocabulary of our internal world is drawn from our "real-world" (external-world) lexicon. So it should come as little surprise to find that even apparently grammatical-function items such as *and* (often analyzed by semanticists as a logical operator devoid of further lexical content) show evidence of ambiguity between uses in the content, epistemic, and speech-act domains. In this section, I will present evidence for the epistemic and speech-act usage of *and, or,* and *but*. My proposal is that not merely the lexical items, but the conjunction process itself, applies analogously in the three domains.

4.2.1   And: *iconic ordering in different domains*

And is, of course, the most general connective in English. Haiman (1980) suggests that many of its apparently multiple meanings may in fact be due to an iconic usage of the general concept of addition or connection. Thus, for example, the *and* of (21) may be simple setting of two items side by side, but that of (22) requires further explanation:

(21a) John eats apples *and* pears.
(21b) King Tsin [a Chinese restaurant] has great mu shu pork *and* China First has good dim sum.
(22)   John took off his shoes *and* jumped in the pool.

In (21a, b) the conveyed meaning would be pretty much unchanged by reversing the order of the conjuncts; but in (22) reversing the order would change our understanding of the order of the represented events (in particular, it might change our opinion as to whether John's shoes got wet or not). Cases like (21a, b) have been called *symmetric* uses of *and*, while (22) is an *asymmetric* use. The asymmetricality of (22) – the fact that we change the interpretation of the sentence if we change the order of the two clauses – is apparently due to the iconic conventions of narrative word-order. The order of the clauses parallels the real-world order of the events described in the clauses, so that it becomes unnecessary to add further specification of the temporal ordering of the events being narrated. *And* does not in itself indicate temporal succession (in the way that such meaning may be attributed to the *then* of *and then*); but the order of two *and*-conjuncts may by convention be iconic for the actual sequence of the events described. I would propose that this narrative usage of *and* is in fact only one of many such ways of exploiting the interaction of language's inherent linearity with the general concept of "putting things side by side."

Let us compare the uses of *and* in (23) and (24):

(23) What happened to Mary?
      Answer: She got an MA in basketweaving *and* she joined a religious cult.
      (...so she left the math department.)

(24) Why don't you want me to take basketweaving again this quarter? *epistemic*
Answer: Well, Mary got an MA in basketweaving, *and* she joined a
religious cult. (...so you might go the same way if you take
basketweaving).

Example (23) is a normal example of iconic narrative word-order, with
and as a connective: it is tacitly assumed that Mary's MA preceded her
joining the religious cult, and the opposite order of events would be the
reasonable interpretation of *She joined a religious cult* and *she got an
MA in basketweaving*. (We also assume that the causality is in accord
with the temporal sequence: earlier events cause later events rather than
vice versa.) But in (24) the clauses are ordered on the basis of a different
principle. Rather than narrative events set side-by-side, here we have
logical premises set side-by-side. The order of the premises is significant,
and the sense would change if they were reversed; the change would not,
however, be one of temporal ordering, but of what was being taken as
logically prior in the epistemic world. Thus, *Well, Mary joined a
religious cult*, and *she got an MA in basketweaving* would indicate that
one could reasonably conclude the likelihood of a basketweaving MA
from somebody's cult membership, while (24) seems rather to be saying
that one concludes the likelihood of cult-joining from the knowledge that
a person has a basketweaving MA.

In example (24) the "*and-so*" sense of *and* is as much a product of iconic
word-order as the "*and-then*" sense (which may also naturally involve
suppositions of real-world causation) of *and* in (23). But the ordering of
(24) is iconic on the logical processes, rather than on the real-world events
involved. That the two clauses of (24) are set side-by-side in a logical world
rather than in an event world is evident from the different conclusions that
can follow (23) and (24). Example (23) can reasonably be followed by a
real-world result of the events previously narrated, while (24) cannot.
Example (24) must, rather, be followed by an epistemic result, a
conclusion which results from the premises previously stated. In no sense
does Mary's life history *cause* my hearer's history to take a parallel course;
rather it causes me to *conclude* that my hearer's history could take the
course in question.

Why should it be the case that epistemic "priority" (such as the priority
of premise over conclusion) should be reflected in iconic word-order in
exactly the same manner as temporal priority of events? Once again, we
can observe the pervasive modeling of our linguistic expression of the
internal world on our expression of the external "real" world. Note that

in this case we have evidence from the lexicon to motivate the iconic use of word order in the epistemic domain. Not only the applicability of words such as *priority* to the logical world (etymologically, it means "previous-ness," a sense retained by the adjective *prior*), but the logical-domain uses of such phrases as "A *follows from* B," or "But that doesn't necessarily *follow*" – these usages show the conception of logical priority drawing its vocabulary from the domain of temporal order. Our examination of epistemic *and*-conjunction has simply shown that more than the lexicon is "borrowed" from the domain of temporality to express logical priority; conventions of word order may be borrowed as well.

And may also connect epistemic entities without any particular asymmetry or priority, in a manner analogous to the content conjunction in (21a, b). In (25) the premises conjoined by *and* are simply set side-by-side as coequal pieces of evidence for some conclusion; no premise has an *and-so* relationship with another.

(25) Did Mary leave for London last night?
Well, nobody has phoned from England to ask why she didn't come, *and* her suitcases are gone, *and* John said he taught her French 2 section for her this afternoon.
(Conclusion: Yes, she went.)

And has thus both content-domain and epistemic-domain usages. In the content domain, our conventions of narrative word-order decree that setting things side-by-side with *and* may further allow their order in the narrative to be an icon for real-world temporal order; real-world causality may also be (secondarily) implied, because we know that earlier events can exert causal force on later ones but not vice versa. In the epistemic domain, setting things side-by-side also allows their order to be taken as iconic under certain circumstances; but it is an icon of logical precedence (the only ordering relevant to the atemporal epistemic domain), rather than of temporal precedence.

And conjoins speech acts as well as content items or logical premises; consider examples (26)–(30):

(26) Go to bed now! *and* no more backtalk!
(27) Glad to meet you, sir; *and* what makes you think I can be of assistance to your work?
(28) Thank you, Mr Lloyd, *and* please just close the door as you go out.
(29) Darling, you're wonderful, *and* how about dinner at Chez Panisse tonight?
(30) The Vietnam War WAS morally wrong, *and* I'll gladly discuss the reasons why I think so.

logical order ~~a~~ parallels that of temporal order

In examples (26)–(29), the mere form of the conjuncts betrays the fact that normal content-domain conjunction cannot be involved. In example (30) grammatical form[7] does not tell us definitely in which domain the two clauses are conjoined. But, given the stress and intonation pattern of the first clause, it has to be interpreted as meaning something like "I *hereby assert again* (or *insist on asserting*) that the Vietnam War was morally wrong." This reading, in fact, conjoins much more reasonably with the content of the second clause than a straightforward content-conjunction reading would: the structure of the conjoined sentence is now "*I assert* that X and *I propose* that we discuss X." Without the stress, the first clause might have quite a different reading, as can be easily seen if we conjoin it to a different second conjunct:

(31) The Vietnam War was morally wrong, *and* its results are still haunting the world today.

Here, content conjunction is involved; the structure is simply "I assert that [X and Y]," where X = "The war was wrong" and Y = "The results still haunt the world."

And has thus (at least) three different domains of application. Not only will the connection between the conjuncts be perceived differently depending on the domain in which they are taken to be conjoined, but the iconic usage of word order will (naturally) be iconic on the ordering principles inherent in the domain in which conjunction takes place (temporal ordering and causality in the real-world domain, but logical priority in the epistemic domain). Many of the multiple interpretations given to *and*-conjunction (including the so-called symmetric vs asymmetric senses) are regular and predictable; given (a) Haiman's concept of iconic word-order, and (b) the understanding that conjunction may be a joining of speech acts or of logical entities rather than a joining of content, these senses are manifestations of the basic sense of setting things side-by-side additively.

It is thus almost certainly unnecessary to postulate multiple semantic senses of *and* to account for the different readings which we began by calling "and then," "and so," etc. First of all, the factors which account for the multiple interpretations of *and*-conjunction are factors which exist in the context, independent of specific lexical semantics. Thus, not only pairs of clauses conjoined with *and*, but also unconjoined clauses in narrative sequence, are interpreted as having an order iconic for the order of events. (Compare *He took off his shoes and jumped in the pool* with the almost equally asymmetrically interpreted *He took off his shoes. He jumped in the pool.*) Second, as pointed out in Horn (1985), it appears to be a crosslinguistic universal that the basic *and*-conjunction in all languages also has asymmetric (e.g., narrative) uses; there is no such thing as a word which means specifically *and* without its narrative senses. This is a further argument against a lexical-polysemy analysis of the different uses of *and*, for the following reasons.

[margin handwritten note: Why not look at a polysemant qualities of and? - the context dictated - could be ordered deliberately - no meaning separate of narrative meanings]

Recall that in discussing the English modal verbs, we said that the root–epistemic polysemy is pervasive, but *not* an absolute requirement for every form with root-modal senses. Similarly, in treating the various uses of English causal conjunctions, we touched on the fact that French has causal conjunctions which are more specialized, sometimes corresponding to sub-uses of Eng. *because*. These facts seem to argue that the multiple interpretations of modal verbs and causal conjunctions may well be facts about the semantics of these individual words. The generalizations about correspondences between root and epistemic senses of these words are thus to be taken as generalizations about polysemy patterns in the semantics of English. We have argued that these regular polysemy patterns in English reflect and are motivated by a broader pattern of metaphorical structuring which is not particular either to English or to these semantic domains; but it is, nonetheless, a fact about lexical semantics that this modal verb has an epistemic sense, just as it is a fact about lexical semantics that one particular verb meaning "see" has acquired "know" as a new sense.

But in the case of *and*, there is no reason to suppose that there is any polysemy relationship between distinguishable senses, since the proposed senses are never, in fact, distinguished by any language. Rather it seems likely that *and* (like negation, as analyzed by Horn [1985]) simply has a sense sufficiently abstract to apply to content, to epistemic actions, and to the ongoing speech-act domain. *And*, then, is not semantically ambiguous but pragmatically ambiguous; its single abstract sense will apply in different ways to the interpretation of the conjuncts, depending on the context.[8]

In arguing that *and* is a unified semantic entity (with a range of systematically related uses), rather than several discrete entities (including perhaps such a divergent sense as temporal conjunction), have we also produced arguments for *what kind* of semantic entity it may be? Grice's (1978) celebrated analysis of *or* showed that by taking account of certain conversational principles, one could simplify the meaning of *or* back down to something fairly closely equivalent to the logical operator ∪. Have we in fact achieved this for *and* and ∩? My answer is that I, at least, don't feel comfortable with such a solution, for two reasons. The first reason is that an equivalence between *and* and ∩ makes more sense when the things conjoined are propositions than when they are epistemic or conversational *actions*. Unless we wish to return to the mechanisms proposed by generative semanticists (see Davison 1973, for example) – in particular, to the inclusion of a higher clause specifying speech-act force as part of the actual semantic content of a sentence – it would be difficult to prove that we are conjoining *propositions* in the examples of *and*-conjunction from the epistemic and speech-act domains. And I feel that the original reasons for abandoning such abstract syntactic analyses were sound.[9] What I hope to do is to catch the real insight which such mechanisms were intended to express (and which has been much neglected by subsequent workers): namely the fact that any utterance simultaneously takes part in several different domains. Without resorting to the mechanism of including essentially pragmatic phenomena in the sentence semantics (or even in the sentence syntax), it is still possible (unless one insists *a priori* on a pragmatics-free semantics) to understand and formulate the relationships between semantics and pragmatics, and the effects of both on interpretation. But it is not immediately obvious that pragmatic entities such as speech-act forces should be formalized as propositions in the same way that linguistic content is formalized – and therefore it is not obvious that *conjoining* such entities is equivalent to logical conjunction or disjunction.

My second reason is related to the first. If we assume that the word *and* in language has the *grammatical* function of conjoining linguistic units (including sentences) as coequals, does that necessarily mean that its *semantic* function is precisely that of logically conjoining the content of two units?[10] Given that it conjoins at other than the propositional-content level, does that mean that the other uses are relevant to its semantics, or not? This is a difficult question, but it looks simpler when stated from another point of view. Given that *and* has some uses which do not parallel those of the logical operator ∩, as well as some which do, does that mean we should analyze ∩ in terms of *and*, or *and* in terms of ∩? My feeling is that it is a mistake to analyze natural-language words like *and* as being identical to entities of the man-made logical terminology which so clearly derives from natural language (rather than the other way around) and so clearly has needs and purposes distinct from those of natural language.

Whatever "putting things side-by-side" may mean in natural language, it only *sometimes* means something equivalent to ∩. Perhaps the closest we can get to stating the relation between *and* and ∩ is to say that ∩ is a mathematical crystallization of one of the most salient uses of *and*. In the next section, we will examine some of the uses of *or* (including some uses neglected by Grice [1978]), and some of the same issues will come up.

4.2.2   Or: Alternatives and conversational structure

Or, frequently analyzed as a logical operator equivalent to ∪, has the same sort of ambiguity between domains as *and*. Its basic meaning seems to be that of conjoining alternatives; these alternatives are normally taken as jointly filling all possible options, so that one or another of them must be the right alternative. In the content domain, conjoining with *or* thus indicates that some one of the conjuncts must describe the genuine state of affairs in the real world.

(32) Every Sunday, John eats pancakes *or* fried eggs.
(On a given Sunday, either "John is eating pancakes" or "John is eating fried eggs" describes the situation truthfully.)
(33) Mary will go to the grocery store this evening, *or* John will go tomorrow morning.
(Either "Mary will go" or "John will go" truthfully describes the future state of affairs.)

Notice that, in contrast with the logical operator ∪, *or* normally carries with it an *expectation* that *only one* of the expressed options will in fact be the correct one. It would not be impossible to say (32) if John sometimes had fried eggs alongside his pancakes, and (33) would not be false if two trips to the grocery store occurred. But (32) and (33) do not create such expectations. Further, it would be absolutely aberrant to say (32) if we knew that John always had eggs and pancakes together – although, from a logical-operator analysis, (32) would, of course, be true. As Grice (1975, 1978) has pointed out, this aberrance is conversational. Our conversational maxims require us to be as informative as necessary; under many circumstances, such informativeness is not provided by the presentation of two or more disjunct possibilities, or at least it would be much more effectively provided by the presentation of one single certainty. Therefore, the statement of disjunct possibilities causes the conversational implicature that the speaker (who presumably would be more helpful, hence more specific, if it were possible) does not know which of the possibilities is correct. Grice does not mention the fact, but *a fortiori* his solution also explains why hearers of disjuncts assume that it is not the case that both possibilities are correct; if the speaker had any good basis for the statement "X *and* Y," to state "X *or* Y" would be at least as uninformative as it would be in the case where the speaker simply knows that "X."

The epistemic use of *or* is exemplified in (34) and (35):

(34) John is home, *or* somebody is picking up his newspapers.
     (reading: The only possible *conclusions* I can reach from the evidence are (a) that John is home to pick up his newspapers, or (b) that somebody is picking them up for him.)
(35) John will be home for Christmas, *or* I'm much mistaken in his character.
     (reading: The only possible conclusions I can reach from the evidence are (a) that John will come home, or (b) that I don't understand his character at all.)

Actually, (34) *could* also be given a content reading: something like "At any given time, it is the case that John is at home, or it is the case that somebody picks up his newspapers for him." But the epistemic reading given in the gloss above, wherein the conjuncts are seen as alternative conclusions drawn from the available evidence rather than as alternative possible real-world states, is surely the likeliest reading. It would be hard to imagine an intelligible content-conjunction reading for (35): the two clauses don't express normal real-world alternatives, but they do express normal epistemic alternatives. A proposed prediction about somebody's future behavior is presumed to be based on some comprehension of the person's character, and hence an alternative to the prediction's validity would be the speaker's poor understanding of the subject's character. However, since we don't usually offer predictions with the intention that they be thought incorrect (again, for Gricean reasons), the speaker cannot cooperatively be offering genuine alternatives here. The assumption made by any hearer of this apparent violation will be that the prediction does reflect the speaker's real conclusion. The second clause, which by itself would have no informational value to the hearer, would (if true) further violate the Gricean maxims by stating that the speaker doesn't know what he/she is talking about. The cooperative hearer, noting that *or* allows a choice of alternatives, will have no trouble deciding that a cooperative speaker must have intended the first clause as the "right" alternative, and the second clause as the "wrong" one. Why would the speaker have bothered to say (35)? It is true that a simpler "John will be home for Christmas" follows logically from (35) plus the conversational maxims.

But (35) is a stronger statement, in that it *explicitly* as well as implicitly puts the speaker on the spot and says "I'm willing to believe myself an incompetent reasoner if what I conclude is not correct."

Finally, *or* can conjoin speech acts, as in (36) and (37):

(36) Have an apple turnover, *or* would you like a strawberry tart?
(37) King Tsin has great mu shu pork, *or* China First has good dim sum, *or* there's always the Szechuan place just around the corner.

Notice that in (36) and (37) there is no possibility of either an epistemic or a content reading of the conjunction. In (36) the imperative and interrogative forms of the conjuncts assure us that only speech-act conjunction can be involved: the hearer is either to take the speaker's speech-act force as suggesting (via a polite imperative) that the hearer eat an apple turnover, *or* as suggesting (via a yet-politer interrogative) that the hearer eat a strawberry tart. Of course, because of the nature of language, both conjuncts have to be *said*, in order for the hearer to choose between them – so, in a way, both speech acts have been carried out by the speaker. But they are presented as alternatives, in that the hearer can choose which of them will form the basis for a response – it is not necessary to respond to both conjuncts. In (37) the declarative form of the conjuncts makes the speech-act conjunction at first less obvious, but there is no sensible reading wherein the conjuncts of (37) are real-world alternatives, or even reasonable alternate conclusions in the speaker's epistemic world (the example makes sense only when read assuming that the speaker treats all conjuncts as true). Only when we see all three conjuncts of (37) as conveyed *suggestions*, can we get a reasonable reading which involves alternatives – the hearer is requested to respond to one or another of the suggestions that "We should go to X restaurant" (which are being conveyed by mentions and commendations of the relevant restaurants).

It is worth noting that (37) is evidence of explicit lexical conjunction linking *indirect* speech-acts; there are no other "alternatives" for *or* to be marking, besides these indirect suggestions. Speech-act conjunction apparently doesn't need to distinguish direct from indirect speech-acts. It is also perhaps worth comparing (37) with (21b), where the first two clauses of (37) are conjoined with *and*. With *and*, a perfectly reasonable content-conjunction reading of these two clauses is possible ("King Tsin has great mu shu pork" and "China First has good dim sum" can be true simultaneously). Of course, the resulting conjunction of contents could, as a conjoined entity, be used as an indirect speech-act – e.g., as a suggestion that we eat at one of the two places. But if we added the third conjunct of (37) to our string of *and*-conjuncts, we would have (37a), which almost forces a speech-act-conjunction interpretation of the *and* because the conventional suggestion force of "there's always" gives the third conjunct an independent status as a suggestion:

(37a) King Tsin has great mu shu pork, *and* China First has good dim sum, *and* there's always the Szechuan place just around the corner.

Does word order play a part in the interpretation of *or*-conjunction, as it does with *and*? In fact, it plays a prominent part, and iconicity may be involved in this case, as with *and*. R. Lakoff (1971) mentions the asymmetric use of *or*, which can be contrasted with a symmetric use. In fact, as with *and*, these two uses are possible in more than one domain of conjunction. Thus, in the content domain, we can contrast the symmetric (38) with the asymmetric (39):

(38a) On Friday nights Mary goes to the movies in Berkeley(,) *or* (she) drives to Tahoe to see Fred.
(38b) On Friday nights Mary drives to Tahoe to see Fred(,) *or* (she) goes to the movies in Berkeley.
(39a) On Friday nights Mary goes to see her aunt, or her parents call her and scold her on Saturday morning.
(39b) *Mary's parents call and scold her on Saturday morning, or on Friday nights she goes to see her aunt.

In the symmetric (38), the two alternatives are mutually exclusive but independent and equivalent to each other (two things Mary could do on Friday evening, not linked except by mutual exclusiveness). But in the asymmetric (39), the second alternative depends on the first, rather than being an independent and equivalent item. It would be perfectly possible for both events to take place; the *either–or* situation does not have to do with either mutual exclusiveness or incomplete information. Rather, our interpretation is that Mary's visit to her aunt will cause the potential subsequent scolding to be averted. In examples of asymmetric-*or* content conjunction like (39), the independent conjunct must always precede the dependent conjunct. This could be said to follow a general principle of iconicity, in that (a) the independent conjunct is causally prior, and (b) in this case, and in most such cases, the independent conjunct has to refer to a temporally prior event, in order for the necessary causal relations to hold. The asterisk in (39b) does not indicate ungrammaticality, but inappropriateness; in order to interpret it as a normal utterance, we would have to interpret the causal chain in a less likely way, so that Mary's parents' not scolding her on Saturday (perhaps the preceding Saturday?) could enable or cause a visit to her aunt on Friday.

In the epistemic domain, asymmetric (41) contrasts with symmetric (40):

(40) A: Yesterday was the day you were supposed to get the decision about that job you applied for.
   B: Yeah. Well, (evidently) the mail delayed it, *or* they got held up making their decision, *or* there was some problem...
(41) (looking at six boxes of pancake mix in John's kitchen cupboard) John eats pancakes for breakfast, *or* I'm the Shah of Iran.

In (40) any of the *or*-conjuncts is an equally possible conclusion in the speaker's epistemic world – and, in fact, more than one might be possible simultaneously. The reading of (40) is something like "I conclude that the evidence leaves me with a set of alternative conclusions: X, or Y, or Z, at least one of which is right." Example (41), on the other hand, doesn't really have equal, independently possible conjuncts. As in (35), the alternatives are one reasonable conjunct and one Griceanly impossible conjunct (given that the speaker and hearer are assumed to know that the speaker is not in fact the Shah of Iran). But, being cooperative, the hearer will understand the message, which is "The only alternative to this conclusion is *absurdity* – hence the conclusion is very strongly supported." And, being likewise cooperative, the speaker doesn't *begin* by stating the absurdity which is simply the non-alternative to his certainty, but by stating the certainty itself. From the point of view of priority in the epistemic world, this word order is equally reasonable; the "I'm the Shah of Iran" clause is only a highly contingent member of the represented epistemic world, irrelevant except as it may serve to reinforce the only real conclusion which the sentence presents. In (40) the speaker might well reason normally from the falsity of one conjunct to the truth of some other, starting from almost any conjunct without much affecting the meaning: "Well, if the mail didn't delay it, (then) they (probably) got held up making their decision" – or, "Well, if they didn't get held up making their decision, (then) the mail (probably) delayed it" are equally possible. Hence the ordering of the *or*-conjuncts is equally flexible; none of them has epistemic dependency on another. But in the case of (41), the second clause is secondary because it lacks any independent value in the reasoning process, serving only to reinforce the first clause. It is true that technically the logical structure of (41) is identical to that of (40) – the falsity of either

conjunct compels the reasoner to conclude the truth of the other;
however, this equality is only apparent in (41), and the speech-act
structure is essentially "John eats pancakes for breakfast," with the *or*-
conjunct added to reinforce the real conclusion.

In the speech-act domain, symmetric uses of *or* such as (36) and (37)
contrast with asymmetric uses like those in (42)–(45):

(42) Happy birthday! *or* did I get the date wrong?
(43) How about coming over this evening? *or* haven't you got the car running
     YET?
(44) Your money *or* your life!
(45) Give me liberty *or* give me death!

As R. Lakoff (1971) points out, asymmetric examples like (45) have
apparent symmetric parallels like (46):

(46a) Give me a hotdog *or* a salami sandwich.
(46b) Give me a salami sandwich *or* a hotdog.

In my opinion, the explanation for the contrast between (45) and (46) is
fairly simple. In (46) the *or* conjoins independent coequal possibilities –
the hearer is really being asked to respond to one speech act or the other.
But in (45) the request for death (a maximally unbelievable and absurd
speech act) *depends* on the prior failure of the maximally reasonable
previous request for liberty. Thus, as in (39), the speaker is indeed
presenting alternatives – but not independent ones. Similarly, the speaker
of (42) has no desire for a response to "did I get the date wrong?" unless
in fact the *real* speech act ("Happy birthday!") is a failure because it's not
the right day. And the speaker of (43) might well not even care about the
state of the car, as long as the hearer is somehow able to accept the
invitation for the evening. The primary, independent conjunct precedes
the secondary, dependent conjunct. In all the asymmetric cases of speech-
act *or*-conjunction that I have been able to find, the secondary dependent
conjunct is subordinate in the Gricean schema: it either gives the speaker
a "loophole" against potential infelicity (as in [42] and [43]), or bolsters
the primary conjunct by presenting an unacceptable alternative (as in [44],
[45], or [47]):

(47) Give me that book, *or* I'll throw your cat into the lake.

The hearer of (47) is asked to choose between responding appropriately to
the initial command "Give me that book," or having the second speech-
act force (the ensuing threat) come into effect. Since the hearer presumably

cannot possibly want the threat, the result is in principle just a strengthened command. But if the initial, primary speech-act force fails or is infelicitous, then the second speech-act force will be the alternative.

All cases of *or*-conjunction, then, present alternatives at some level – in the content domain, in the speaker's epistemic domain, or in the conversational domain. The presentation of alternatives (as mentioned earlier) commonly carries with it the conversational implicature that *both* (or all) alternatives are *not* simultaneously correct. Hence, mutual exclusiveness of the different options is a frequent default interpretation of *or*-sentences, although it is not a necessary interpretation of most of them. However, in order for an *or*-conjoined utterance to be conversationally cooperative at all, it must be interpreted as offering the hearer *at least* one correct option. Independent options are presented with "symmetric" *or* – that is, the ordering of the conjuncts is irrelevant. For two independent options, of which at least one is true, it would be as reasonable to say "If not B, then A" as to say "If not A, then B." The free ordering of the *or*-clauses reflects the lack of priority of one option over the other.

If, however, the two options are not independent of each other, then another factor enters the picture. "Asymmetric" *or* reflects the dependence of one of the alternatives on the other. The two conjuncts still need not be mutually exclusive in themselves – that is, when I say "Mary gets home by midnight, *or* her parents are furious," I don't mean that the two events described *could not* both occur. But I am implying that there is a one-way relationship between them. Taking "Mary gets home by midnight" as A, and "her parents are furious" as B, we can (as always with *or*-conjunction) reason either "If not A, then B" or "If not B, then A." However, in the real world, we know that A (Mary's time of coming home) is not only temporally prior, but actually exerts a *causal* influence on B (her parents' furiousness). And we know that the converse cannot be true: in no way can her parents' subsequent furiousness influence the time of her previous homecoming. Note that from the point of view of epistemic *or*-conjunction, it would actually be possible to reverse the two conjuncts – e.g., "Mary's parents are furious (now), or (else) she got home by midnight." Here, since real-world alternatives are not at issue (one or the other already is in effect), only epistemic alternatives can be in question; and neither one has definite priority over the other, in the way that one real-world alternative causally controls the other.

My hypothesis, then, is that the order of asymmetric *or*-conjuncts reflects the priority of one conjunct over the other, or the dependency of the second on the first. This dependency may be at the content level (not-A controls or causes B in the real world), the epistemic level (A is a real conclusion, and B is only presented as a non-alternative in support of A), or the speech-act level (the infelicity or poor success of speech-act force A would cause me to replace it with speech-act force B) – we have seen examples of all three. In all cases the independent, primary conjunct precedes the dependent, secondary conjunct, in what might be easily seen as another example of iconic word-order.

A final question regarding *or* is, naturally, whether Grice (1978) was correct in reducing its semantics back down to ∪. I do not dispute his explanation of the conversational implicature of *or*-sentences; as has been seen, I rely on it as the basis for my more extended account of *or*. As in the case of *and*, however, it becomes strained to imagine logical conjunction or disjunction of epistemic and conversational actions. It seems more reasonable to view the logical *or* as a neatly trimmed *piece* of the natural-language *or*'s semantics, whittled to fit philosophers' needs, than to see ∪ as the basic semantics of the word *or*.

4.2.3   But: *epistemic and conversational conflict*

The semantics of *but* are the final subject of this chapter. *But* presents two conjuncts which clash with each other in some way – it is contrary to our expectations to see the two presented side-by-side. The clash can occur in at least two of the three domains we have previously mentioned. At the epistemic level, the available premises may clash with an apparently necessary conclusion (as in [48]), or with other apparent premises (as in [49]):

(48) John keeps six boxes of pancake mix on hand, *but* he never eats pancakes.
     (The premise that he stocks pancake mix would lead me to the conclusion
     that he's a pancake-eater, which clashes with the otherwise well-evidenced
     conclusion that he never touches a pancake.)
(49) Do you know if Mary will be in by nine this evening?
     Answer: Well, she's nearly always in by then, *but* (I know) she has a lot
     of work to do at the library, so I'm not sure.
     (The two premises, "Mary's usually in by then" and "Mary has lots of
     library work" clash in that the first supports the conclusion that Mary
     will be in by nine, while the second supports the conclusion that she will
     not.)

At the conversational level, apparently clashing speech acts may be conjoined with *but*:

(50) (Please) look up that phone number – *but* don't bother if it will take you *– conditional*
more than a few minutes.
(One speech act requests or commands the hearer to do something; the
other countermands the order, albeit conditionally.)

(51) King Tsin has great mu shu pork, *but* China First has excellent dim sum. *offering choice*
(The initial indirect suggestion of going to eat at King Tsin apparently
clashes with the subsequent indirect suggestion of going to eat at China
First; both suggestions cannot, presumably, be followed simultaneously.)

The use of *but* in (50) and (51) signals the speaker's consciousness of
presenting two at least partially discordant speech acts side-by-side. In
both cases there are good reasons – the speaker is not simply being self-
contradictory. Example (50), with its conditional countermanding of an
order, simply results in a conditional speech-act equivalent to "Please
look up that phone number if it won't take you too long"; I will discuss
conditional speech-acts in some detail in the next chapter. Example (51)'s
apparent clash of alternatives is in fact just one way of offering the hearer
options which are acknowledged as mutually exclusive. It is politer to
present such options, and allow the hearer to choose among them (see R.
Lakoff 1972b, 1973) than to offer only one of the possibilities. Since both
suggestions must be performed in order for the hearer to choose, the result
is an apparent self-contradiction by the speaker, who seems to be
simultaneously proposing two mutually exclusive options.

Notice that there can be no question of epistemic conjunction or
content conjunction in (50) or (51). In (50) the imperative force tells us
that we are dealing with conjoined speech-acts. In (51) there is no clash
between the conjuncts in the content domain (the speaker doesn't mean
that there is any problem for the simultaneous existence of both
restaurants, with menus as described) or in the epistemic domain (the
speaker doesn't mean that it is hard to simultaneously *believe* both
statements); only the conveyed speech-act forces of suggestion clash with
one another.

A more complicated speech-act use of *but* is discussed in R. Lakoff
(1971):

(52) George likes mu shu pork, *but* so do all linguists.

The interpretation of this sentence is as follows. I tell you that George
likes mu shu pork; a normal speech-act implicature of my telling you
something is that I assume you don't already know it or I don't consider
it obvious. This implicature clashes with my subsequent statement that all

linguists like mu shu pork, because that statement (given George's identity as a linguist) implies that I think it *is* obvious that George likes mu shu pork. In this case I have just taken away the basic conversational justification for the *first* of the two conjoined speech acts. Once again, as in the cases of (50) and (51), there may be good reasons for this apparent clash of purposes. For example, the speaker may not *want* to appear too Griceanly informative (e.g., for fear of seeming officious); or the speaker's entire purpose may be, not to present a fact and then take away its interest, but to *comment* on the obviousness of the fact. Nonetheless, the apparent clash remains; and conjunction with *but* marks the clash.

The obvious question which I have left unaddressed is whether there is a content usage of *but*. Every other conjunction we have seen has had a basic content-domain usage, alongside extended uses in the epistemic and speech-act domains. Why should *but* be different? It is hard to answer this question definitively one way or the other. I have already noted that we frequently tend to reason from known real-world effect to likely real-world cause; but, of course, we also often reason from known real-world event (a potential cause) to probable real-world effect of that cause. In section 4.1 on causal conjunction, I mentioned the frequent apparent ambiguity between epistemic-domain and content-domain causal conjunction, which is caused by the expression of the latter mode of reasoning. Comma intonation helps to disambiguate in certain cases between causal conjunction in the two domains:

(53a) He's going to marry her because he loves her.
(Only reading: real-world causation of the marriage by love.)
(53b) He's going to marry her, because he loves her.
(Ambiguous: *either* real-world causation as in (a) but with assertion of the first clause, *or* (more likely) the *knowledge* of the love causes the *conclusion* that the marriage will happen.)

Less ambiguity usually results from epistemic causal-conjunction when it reflects effect-to-cause reasoning, but even then we can usually find a pragmatic context which would allow us to give a content-conjunction reading. All we need to do is presume real-world causality to be reversed.

(54) He loves her, because he's going to marry her.

The most likely interpretation of (54) is "I conclude that he loves her, because I know he's going to marry her" – but if we can bring ourselves to conceive of engagement causing love in the real world, we can also get a successful content reading for *because*.

Returning to the problem of *but*, it is true that many *but*-examples might, *prima facie*, seem connected with "real-world" clash or contrast. Thus, for example, cases like (55) or (56) might at least have initial credibility if put forward as examples of content-*but*:

(55) John eats pancakes regularly, *but* he never keeps any flour or pancake mix around.
(56) John is rich but Bill is poor.

Now, in (55) John's eating pancakes might lead him to stock the relevant ingredients in the real world; hence we could say that there is a clash, in that a normal real-world causal sequence seems disrupted. The problem is that we could equally easily claim that the clash is epistemic. The naturalness of a pancake-eater's stocking flour would lead us to *conclude* from John's habits that he stocks flour. However, this conclusion clashes with the (otherwise well-supported) fact that he doesn't stock flour. How can we prove that content conjunction is involved? We have, on the other hand, clear evidence elsewhere for epistemic conjunction with *but*; cases like (48) and (49) do not readily admit of a content-conjunction reading. What about (56)? At what level does John's richness clash with Bill's poverty? There is no bar in the real world to the simultaneous existence of poor and rich people. In the epistemic domain, there is likewise no initially obvious intrinsic clash, in that we can perfectly well *believe* in both John's wealth and Bill's poverty simultaneously. It would be possible to say simply (57), however, if no clash or contrast were intended between the two clauses:

(57) John is rich *and* Bill is poor.

The *but* in (56) does indeed indicate contrast: an epistemic contrast between two semantically opposed propositions. They are not *contradictory* propositions (note the impossibility of [58]), but they involve opposite logical structures (A and $\sim$ A, *rich* and *poor*).

(58) *John is rich but he is poor.

Having said all this, I am still not sure I want to state categorically that there is no such thing as a content-domain use of *but*. However, I have not been able to unearth any indubitable content-conjunction examples with *but*. And in fact there seems to be a plausible explanation for the use of *but* in only two domains, while other conjunctions are used in three. Causation, side-by-side copresence, and either–or status actually exist in all three domains. That is to say, in the real world A may cause B, or A and B may coexist, or A and B may be the only possible alternative outcomes of a given real-world situation. But what does it mean to say that A and B "clash" or "contrast" in the real world? How can discordance or contrast exist outside of the speaker's mental concept of harmony or non-contrast? In a sense, if two states coexist in the real world (and conjunction with *but* does present both conjuncts as true), then they cannot be said to clash at a real-world level. A sentence like (59) does not really express a contrast between real-world Catholicism and real-world socialism, but rather the speaker's beliefs about the likelihood of the two coexisting.

(59) France is Catholic *but* socialist. (said during Mitterand's government)
   (Clash between (a) my belief that Catholic countries aren't usually socialist, so that I normally reason from Catholicism to capitalism, and (b) my knowledge that France, nonetheless, is socialist.)

So, for the moment, I see no reason to conclude that *but* has a content-domain usage, and indeed I see some naturalness to the idea that it lacks such a usage.[11]

Of course, contrast inheres in our conversational goals, quite as easily as in our epistemic world *per se*. We have seen examples of conversational goals which are seen as conflicting, and noted that conjoined speech acts bearing such conflicting goals are conjoined with *but*. The conversational world, being a mental world like our world of reasoning, includes speakers' judgments as to what conflicts with what. Sometimes only pragmatic context can tell us in which of the two mental domains the contrast is being presented to us. Thus the ambiguity of (50) is noted by R. Lakoff (1971), who calls the two senses *opposition* and *denial of expectation*:

(60) John is rich but dumb. *opposition*

Lakoff's "denial of expectation" sense of (60) is the reading in which someone is assumed to have previously asserted that rich people are usually smart (that's how they got rich), and John is being produced as a counterexample to this normal expectation. This can be seen as an example of epistemic *but*-conjunction (in my normal train of reasoning, a belief in someone's intelligence would follow from my knowing the person to be rich – but this train of reasoning conflicts with the otherwise well-supported fact that John (a rich man) is dumb.)

Lakoff's "opposition" sense of (60), on the other hand, is one in which someone is proposing or evaluating John for some purpose (e.g., as a possible husband). Here, John's richness and stupidity need not have any connection with each other in the real world or in the logical world (I need not be able to draw conclusions about either one from the other); but they are in conflict because his wealth suggests that it would be a good idea to marry him, while his stupidity suggests the reverse. This is a case of what I have called speech-act or conversational *but*-conjunction; the two clauses conveying the two opposed speech acts "I suggest that you marry him" and "I suggest that you not marry him" are conjoined, and the perceived conflict between them is expressed by the use of *but*. Notice, as we observed earlier in (51), that speech-act conjunction in (60) does not conjoin *direct* (surface) forces; the *conveyed* speech-act forces are recognized as contrasting, and it is therefore the conveyed suggestion-forces of the two conjuncts that are conjoined with *but*.[12]

The contrast between symmetric and asymmetric *but* is given perhaps the fullest treatment of any subject touched on in Lakoff's paper. She is not particularly classifying in terms of a (content vs) epistemic vs speech-act division of domains, but much of what she says in her analysis of symmetry and asymmetry can be carried over into the analysis of *but* which I have just given. Her basic generalization, despite problematic cases which she discusses at length, is that "opposition" *but* is symmetric, while "denial of expectation" *but* is asymmetric. This generalization does seem to hold, and I think that my preceding analysis in fact affords us the necessary background for an explanation of *why* it should hold.

Lakoff's "semantic opposition" *but* in fact corresponds to cases where the two conjuncts are presented as equal and independent, but conflicting or contrasting – for example, "John is rich but Bill is poor" as an epistemic contrast, or "King Tsin has great mu shu pork, but China First has excellent dim sum" as a clash between conflicting speech-act forces. In these cases, either of the two conjuncts could come first, and the interpretation would be essentially the same because they are independent of each other.

Lakoff's "denial of expectation" *but*, on the other hand, corresponds to cases where there is not direct and mutual (coequal) contrast between the two conjuncts, but rather the second conjunct conflicts or contrasts with some implicature *dependent* on the first conjunct. Thus, in the epistemic domain, "John is rich but dumb" might express a conflict between a supposed chain of reasoning from the fact of John's wealth (to his intelligence) and the actual known fact of John's stupidity. Or in the speech-act domain, "I love you, but PLEASE take those wet boots off the carpet!'" might express a conflict between the supposed expectations set up by a speech act like "I love you," and the actual reproofs which follow. Lakoff actually analyzes one conversational case in some detail – essentially the case of my example (52). After some discussion, she finally, and I believe correctly, decides that this particular example falls under her "denial of expectation" heading: "My saying that George likes mu shu pork might lead you to expect that this is something inobvious enough to deserve declaring, but in fact it's an obvious fact because all linguists like mu shu pork."

In all these asymmetric cases, Lakoff comments that *but* seems to be the contrastive equivalent of an asymmetric *and*; symmetric *but*, on the other hand, she takes to be the contrastive counterpart of symmetric *and*. In one sense, she is right. Symmetric *but*, like *and*, displays two elements side-by-side – with the added feature of contrast or conflict, which need not be present with *and* (although it is not barred from being present in *and*-conjoined sentences). Asymmetric *and* has an *and-then* or an *and-so* sense (only *and-so* in the epistemic domain) – that is to say, it conjoins elements which are either in temporal sequence or in a relationship of causality or logical priority with one another; the temporally or causally or logically prior conjunct must precede the other conjunct. Asymmetric *but* might be taken as the contrastive counterpart to this asymmetric *and*, in that it conjoins a causally or logically prior first conjunct, and a second conjunct which is in *contrast* to the normal result of causal or logical sequence from the first conjunct. (Note that *but* does not have the simple temporal-sequence use that *and* does; presumably this is because we don't have an element of contrast in the temporal/real-world domain, although we do in the other two domains.) That is to say, the second conjunct of an asymmetric *but* is dependent on the first, in that its purpose is to contrast with some "normal" second conjunct which would have a "normal" causal or logical dependency on the first conjunct. Thus, there is a sort of *counter-* "*and-so*" sense to asymmetric *but*. As we have now come to expect, the dependent conjunct (the structural equivalent of the *and-so* clause) must follow the independent conjunct.

Let us take a look at a couple of asymmetric *but* examples before going on to some of Lakoff's problem cases. A parallel to example (24) from section 4.2.1 on *and* is given as (61) below, and (24) is reproduced alongside for comparison.

(61) Well, Mary got an MA in computer science, *but* she joined a religious cult. (...so nothing is a safe field any more.)

(24) Well, Mary got an MA in basketweaving, *and* she joined a religious
cult, ... (so you might go the same way if you take basketweaving).

The common factor in (61) and (24) is that the speakers evidently reason
from the subject of a person's MA *to* the likelihood of that person's joining
a religious cult. Compare (61) and (24) with (62a, b), where the order of the
conjuncts is reversed:

(62a) Well, Mary joined a religious cult, *but* she got an MA in computer
science.
(62b) Well, Mary joined a religious cult, *and* she got an MA in basketweaving.

Examples (62a, b) seem to presume that religious-cult membership is the
prior data from which one reasons to likely MA fields, rather than the
other way around (as in [61] and [24]). In the two *but*-examples, the
consequent is unexpected from the prior data, while in the *and*-examples
it is expected, but in either case it seems clear that the first clause is taken
as prior and the second clause as dependent upon it. Notice that although
but always indicates contrast, the versatile *and* allows the interpretation of
contrasting elements, as well as that of harmonious ones:

(63) Q: What, you don't think even computer science is a safe field?
A: Well, Mary got an MA in computer science, *and* she (went and) joined
a religious cult (just the same).
(64) I've spent weeks doing this report, *but/and* they won't accept it because of
the typos.

Examples (63) and (64) are standard examples of asymmetric *and*, wherein
the first clause is considered to be temporally or causally or logically prior
to the second. However, as is *obligatorily* the case with asymmetric *but*, the
second conjuncts of (63) and (64) show an unlikely or abnormal sequential
relationship to the first clause, rather than a normal sequence. The order
of the clauses still reflects their dependency relationship, whether that
relationship is viewed as normal or aberrant.[13]

Let us return, as promised, to some of R. Lakoff's (1971) problem cases
of *but*. She first remarks on the strangeness of the fact that (65)–(68) are
all acceptable (her examples [71]–[74] are given below as [65]–[68]):

(65) Bill murdered Alice, but he was caught.
(66) Bill murdered Alice, but he got away.
(67) Bill murdered Alice, and he was caught.
(68) Bill murdered Alice, and he got away.

She claims that there must be two types of asymmetric *but*, in order to
account for both (65) and (66). Only one of these two can be the usual

denial-of-expectation *but*, since the two sentences would deny *different* expectations. Lakoff finds (68) only questionably acceptable, stating that (unlike [67]) it requires a special context like a discussion of the prevalence of unpunished crime; she therefore suggests that being caught does *not* run counter to our normal expectations about murderers (hence [67] is more normal than [68]), while getting away *does* run counter to these expectations. Example (66) is thus to be read as a case of denial-of-expectation *but*, while (65) is a case of some other variety of asymmetric *but* (perhaps one "whose asymmetry derives from temporal priority"[14]).

Although I find Lakoff's treatment of (65) and (66) incomplete, her own work (1972b, 1973) and that of Gumperz (1982) have suggested some approaches to this problem. In Lakoff (1972b) she shows in detail, for a set of politeness cases, how speakers' contextualization affects their interpretation of speech acts. Gumperz (1982) contains an explicit discussion of our techniques for creating context by using forms appropriate to the desired context. Just as context and presupposition influence choice of linguistic form, so a chosen form marks the supposed existence of some given context or presupposition – and hence can be deliberately used to evoke that context or to communicate that set of presuppositions. Lakoff (presumably showing faith in the police and the legal system) finds that her normal expectation is that murderers are caught rather than allowed to escape. Hence she finds (67) more normal in a default context than (68). However, she freely admits that a different context would easily make (68) acceptable. My proposed solution to the difficulty of (65) and (66) is to say that the same asymmetric use of *but* occurs in both sentences. However, in one sentence, the speaker is presupposing (or presenting him/herself as presupposing) the normality of a criminal's escape, while in the second, the normality of a criminal's capture is presupposed.[15]

Lakoff also presents as a puzzle the following group of sentences:

(69) John is a doctor today, but he failed chemistry.
(70) John would be a doctor today, but he failed chemistry.
(71) John thought he would be a doctor, but he failed chemistry.
(72) John wanted to be a doctor, but he failed chemistry.
(73) *John managed to be a doctor, but he failed chemistry.
(74) *John realized he would be a doctor, but he failed chemistry.

The first mystery is why the factive verbs *manage* and *realize*, which presuppose the truth of the complement "John is a doctor," should give bad examples ([73] and [74]); while (69), which simply *states* that "John is a doctor," should be a perfectly acceptable sentence. I am by no means convinced that (73) and (74) are impossible sentences (in the way that, e.g., "John is rich but poor" seems impossible in a non-metaphoric reading); however, I agree with Lakoff that their bizarreness needs explanation. In order to try to give such an explanation, I will first turn to the "good" sentences (69)–(72). Lakoff argues that only (69) is an example of denial-of-expectation *but*, while the others are examples of some other variety. The problem with (70)–(72) is that the second clause in these sentences not only does not seem to deny any *rigid* expectation created by the first clause, but it further carries with it the strong implicature that John is *not* a doctor. The second clause in (69) certainly carries no such implication.

My understanding of (70)–(72) is as follows. A statement of John's plans or hopes, or of some expected normal course of events (as in, e.g., "John would be a doctor today"), naturally gives some motivation for a line of reasoning ending in the fulfillment of the expectations: John's becoming a doctor and hence probably passing chemistry along the way. But, of course, such a statement does not give us the *assurance* of John's success which the direct statement in the first clause of (69) automatically provides. When we add "but he failed chemistry" as a second conjunct in (69), there is no possibility of contradicting what is directly stated in the preceding clause (otherwise we would have a "John is rich but poor" clash); so there is assumed to be merely a contradiction of our expectation that John passed chemistry. But in (70)–(72), the line of reasoning to John's success is still only tentative, and the contradiction of one part of his progress towards his goal (failure in chemistry) tends, if unqualified, to make us conclude that his whole medical career failed as well. Such a conclusion is especially well-supported by the normal counterfactual reading of *would* in (70).[16] Note that (72) in particular could more easily escape a counterfactual reading of the first clause. It would be perfectly possible to say "John wanted to be a doctor, but he failed chemistry, and in the end his father had to force him to retake it and bribe him to go on and get his MD."

My conviction is that (73) and (74) need significantly more *context* than (69), but that they are not in themselves ungrammatical or "less grammatical." Consider, for example, a context where John knows that he will have to be a doctor whatever he does – his fate was decided by the government at age ten. His failing chemistry will only result in a longer training period and more frustration along the way, so we would expect him to do his duty to the state and avoid such an eventuality if possible.

Then, it seems to me, (74) is a perfectly acceptable utterance. The reason why (74) is normally unacceptable is that it is hard to find a context where someone's *realization* that he will be a doctor is independent of his passing chemistry; and we know that the first clause of a *but*-conjoined sentence cannot be dependent on the second. Note, conversely, the somewhat greater ease of finding a context for (75), where the dependency of the relevant realization on chemistry grades is appropriately mirrored in the word order:

(75) John failed chemistry; but he realized he would be a doctor, so he retook it in hopes of not killing too many patients.

For (73), which I already consider marginal rather than totally ungrammatical, consider a context wherein the hearer had asked the speaker if John would be a good person to consult on certain medical subjects. Example (73) would, it seems to me, be a normal enough response, and would have the same basic structure as (69). Again, it seems to me that the difficulty lies in creating a context wherein John's "managing" is not taken as dependent (in our reasoning) on his failing or passing chemistry. Note that (76), wherein the dependency relationship is an expected one, given the order of the clauses, is acceptable:

(76) John failed chemistry, but he managed to be a doctor.

Note also that in (69)–(72), the first clause *is* taken as independent of the second: John's hopes, opinions, or default expected career are not dependent on his *subsequent* failing of chemistry, in the way that his ultimate realization of his future, or his success in becoming a doctor, might easily be understood as dependent on his chemistry grades. Nor is his present undisputed status as a doctor (in [69]) dependent on anything at all: such a separate and unqualified assertion seemingly forces us to make the assumption that John's doctorhood is independent of his chemistry grades – an assumption which we apparently had more trouble in making for the presupposition cases of *manage* and *realize* ([73] and [74]).[17]

But is thus used both symmetrically and asymmetrically, in (at least) the epistemic and speech-act domains. In the epistemic domain, the postulated difference between asymmetric and symmetric uses is the difference between coequal premises (or contrasting propositions) and cases where the train of reasoning leads from the first clause to the second clause. In the speech-act domain, the difference is between contrasting or conflicting but coequal speech acts (such as mutually exclusive suggestions) versus cases where the second clause follows from the first (e.g., conditionally supersedes the first) or otherwise depends on the first clause (e.g., crucially refers to the felicity conditions evoked by the first clause).

4.3 Conclusions

The essential point of this chapter has been that we can interpret syntactic conjunction of clauses in three distinct ways: as conjunction of content, as conjunction of premises in the epistemic world, and as conjunction of the speech acts performed via the utterance of the clauses in question. The interpretation actually given to a conjoined pair of clauses is pragmatically determined.

If we add the idea of iconic word-order to this multiple interpretation of conjunction, we can explain most of the differences between symmetric and asymmetric coordinate conjunction. With the basic coordinate conjunctions *and* and *or*, the linear asymmetry of word order is open to iconic interpretation, since there is no inherent asymmetric semantic relation between the conjuncts. With subordinate conjunctions such as *because*, word order can no longer be iconic because the conjunction already expresses an asymmetric relation between the clauses, however they are ordered. The different natures of the content domain and the epistemic domain are reflected in the interpretations given to iconic word-order. The sequence of *and*-conjuncts in the content domain tends to take on an "and-then" reading of temporal sequence, and often a causal reading based on temporal sequence, while the same sequence of conjuncts in the epistemic world takes on an "and-so" reading of logical sequence in reasoning.

Intonational differences between content-domain causal conjunction and epistemic or speech-act causal conjunction fall out from the differences between the content domain and the other two domains. A comma intonation (indicating non-presupposed content of the protasis) is typical of epistemic and speech-act causal conjunction, precisely because a speaker's in-process epistemic and conversational acts are not shared ground between speaker and addressee.

It is important to note that *and* and *or* have often been treated as logical operators (see Horn 1972), hence as the most fundamental evidence for the inherent logical structuring of natural language. This chapter has shown that *and* and *or*, like *but*, and like causal and adversative conjunctions, partake of a much broader set of functions than the logical joining of propositions. In particular, cases where syntactic form clearly shows that speech acts are conjoined (e.g. "Where were you last night(?), and don't give me any nonsense about staying late at the office!" or "Please look up that phone number, but not if it's too much trouble.") would be serious problems for a unified theory of conjunction if propositions alone were thought of as being potential conjuncts. The conjoining of indirect speech-acts is especially interesting, since it appears that speakers can use either the conjunction appropriate to the literal readings of the conjuncts *or* the conjunction appropriate to the conveyed readings. Assuming that an abstract syntactic analysis (higher syntactic predicates of saying, or of concluding) is not an acceptable alternative, only an analysis which takes into account an utterance's multi-domain existence can possibly explain the three pragmatically conditioned interpretations of conjunction in the different domains.

5 Conditionals

Conditionals are a highly controversial subject in current linguistic analysis. This chapter is intended to show how *if–then* conjunction fits into the framework I have described in the preceding chapters, rather than to propose any full theory of conditionals. My analysis will often support some particular view of the phenomenon of conditionality, rather than another, or suggest motivations for previously proposed analyses. But the main object will be simply to elucidate the functioning of conditionality in the content, epistemic, and speech-act domains.[1]

5.1   Conditionals in three domains

5.1.1   *Content conditionals*

The first step is an examination of "real-world" or content-domain conditionals. It has often been observed (see Austin 1961; Haiman 1978, 1986; Comrie 1986) that the natural-language use of conditionals is not in fact identical with the conditionality defined by logical *if–then* ($\supset$). Most obviously, speakers of natural languages reject as bizarre whole classes of logically well-formed and "true" conditionals such as (1):

(1) If Paris is the capital of France, (then) two is an even number. *is true but not very logical*

Logically, a conditional is only false if the antecedent is true but the consequent is false. But natural-language speakers apparently require more than the appropriate truth values in order to accept a conditional as *well-formed*: they require a connection between the two clauses. Natural language uses conditionals to talk about *related* things. Examples like (1) *well-formed clauses* are bizarre because we cannot imagine a relationship between the contents of the protasis and apodosis; under what circumstances would the evenness of two be conditionally dependent on or related to Paris' being the capital of France? Van der Auwera (1986) argues in favor of the "Sufficient Conditionality Thesis" i.e., *if p, then q* means "p is a sufficient condition of q." Despite some problems with Van der Auwera's analysis (we will see later that his definition needs to be broadened to deal with concessives), I will accept this hypothetical definition as a starting point. Such a view is structurally similar to the one held by Gazdar (1979) and Stalnaker (1968), that conditionals simply mean that the consequent is true in every case where the antecedent is true. However, it differs in assuming a *connection* between the truth of the antecedent and the truth of the consequent.

In the content domain, then, conditional *if–then* conjunction indicates that the realization of the event or state of affairs described in the protasis is a sufficient condition[2] for the realization of the event or state of affairs described in the apodosis. Thus (2) means that if the real-world state of affairs includes Mary's going, then it will also include John's going:

(2) If Mary goes, John will go.

Here the connection between antecedent and consequent may be a causal one; Mary's going might bring about or enable John's going, or Mary's not going could in some way cause John's not going.

Depending on the pragmatic context and the linguistic form, the fulfillment of the sufficient condition presented in the protasis may appear more or less likely. Comrie (1986) gives an excellent argument that counterfactual conditionals are not in fact really counterfactual, nor are "ordinary" hypothetical conditionals inherently non-counterfactual. Pragmatic context can reverse the effects of supposedly counterfactual verb-forms; for example, either (3) or (4) could be used as a way of getting the hearer to bring the speaker some coffee:

(3) If you get me some coffee, I'll give you a cookie.
(4) If you got some coffee, I'd give you a cookie.

Example (4) certainly represents the protasis as being less likely than (3) does, but neither version is counterfactual. However, in many contexts, verb forms such as those used in (4) would be understood as pragmatically indicating counterfactuality, as in (5):

(5) If I were president, I'd sell the White House's Limoges china to fund bilingual education.

Given that the speaker is *known* not to be the president,[3] the use of the past-tense verb in the protasis and the conditional modal *would* in the apodosis may be interpreted with certainty as counterfactual markers, whereas (as we have seen in [4]) their literal linguistic import is simply that of dubitativeness, marking a high degree of hypotheticality.

Whatever the degree of hypotheticality, the relationship marked by *if–then* remains the same: the fulfillment of the protasis, likely or unlikely, is a sufficient condition for the fulfillment of the apodosis. In content conjunction, this often means that there is assumed to be a causal relationship between the two, as in (2), where the most likely interpretation is probably that Mary's going (if it occurs) will *cause* John to decide to go. Equally, there may be a negative causal relationship involved: for example, one could take (2) as meaning that Mary's *not* going would somehow prevent John's going, although her going would not be an active cause in making him decide to go too. Example (5) is most easily read this way: it is the speaker's not being president which prevents his/her selling the White House china, although being president would not *cause* the sale in question. In these cases, the fulfillment of the antecedent condition is rather an *enablement* than a cause of the consequent; and the enablement is further viewed as being sufficient to assure the consequent's fulfillment – i.e, in (5) the will involved in making the decision is already committed, so no further positive causality is needed, and enablement suffices. Enablement and causation are linguistically treated as identical with respect to conditionals, as they often are elsewhere (see section 4.1 on causal conjunction). But either a hypothetical enablement or a hypothetical cause may be a sufficient antecedent for the fulfillment of some consequent event or condition.

A frequently observed fact about *if* is that it is often read as "if and only if" ("iff") – that is, a common reading of *if–then* conjunction is one wherein the protasis is taken as being not merely a sufficient but a *necessary* condition for the apodosis. Many of the preceding examples easily receive this reading as a default interpretation. Comrie (1986) argues convincingly, however, that this "if and only if" reading of *if* is not part of the semantics of *if*, but is rather a conversational implicature which easily follows from the sufficient-conditionality use of *if*. Take, for example, a sentence such as (2):

(2) If Mary goes, John will go.

It is not impossible, upon hearing (2), to imagine that subsequently John could go even though Mary stays home. But one very obvious interpretation of (2) is that John (a) will go if Mary goes, *and* (b) won't go if Mary doesn't. Comrie argues that (b) follows conversationally from the statement of (a) in many circumstances. Suppose, for example, that I want John to go: (2) would suggest to me that Mary's going will bring about what I want. Presumably, however, the speaker would not have *bothered* to tell me that Mary's going will ensure John's going, if there were a reasonable likelihood of John's going anyway. For example, if John's going were certain and Mary's doubtful (in which case [2] would still be a perfectly well-formed *logical if–then*), there would be no point at all in stating (2). Thus there is a conversational implicature that John is at least unlikely to go if Mary doesn't go. This conversational implicature is cancellable: imagine the case where I'm interested in catching Mary alone without John, rather than in ensuring John's going. In that case, (2) may be uttered with little or no chance of receiving an iff interpretation; it will be quite irrelevant what John's independent habits are, and the statement will simply be taken as meaning that Mary's going will ensure John's going – hence there is no chance that Mary will be the only one going. Particularly in cases like (3) and (4), where the speaker is attempting to get the hearer to do something ("If you do X, I'll do Y"), there would be little point to the conversation if the speaker intended to do Y whether or not the hearer did X. The conversational implication must be that the speaker would *not* normally do Y. The normal interpretation of such sentences is thus "I'll do Y if and only if you do X." I take examples such as these to be fairly solid evidence that the "if and only if" reading is not part of the inherent semantics of *if*, but rather a frequent default conversational interpretation of *if–then* conditional sentences.

if and only if → interp. determined by conversational implications

5.1.2   Epistemic conditionals

In the epistemic domain, *if–then* conjunction expresses the idea that knowledge of the truth of the hypothetical premise expressed in the protasis would be a sufficient condition for concluding the truth of the proposition expressed in the apodosis.

(6) If she's divorced, (then) she's been married.

needless repetition

The tautological conditional expressed in (6) might be read as follows: the knowledge that the proposition "she's divorced" is true is a sufficient condition to ensure my concluding that "she has been married" is also true. A non-tautological epistemic conditional is expressed in (7):

(7) If John went to that party, (then) he was trying to infuriate Miriam.

In (7) there is no inherent linguistic or logical connection between protasis and apodosis. Presumably the speaker has a general, tacitly assumed data-base; and the addition to that data-base of the truth of "John went to that party" will suffice to allow the conclusion that the proposition "he was trying to infuriate Miriam" is also true.

Note that this analysis of epistemic conditionals is *formally* parallel (as is the preceding discussion of content-level conditionals) to a treatment which assumes that *if a, then b* means "when a is true, b is always true." However, even under such an analysis, one would still have to gloss (7) as "When a reasoner *knows* that John went to the party, that reasoner always *concludes* that he went to infuriate Miriam." Even this gloss is slightly odd – it is not enough to recognize that the conditionality is between epistemic states rather than between propositions, it is further necessary to assume some connection between knowledge and conclusion. The causal link involved in (7) is certainly not at the content level, but is easy to see at the epistemic level – the knowledge causes the conclusion.[4]

Epistemic conditionals are, not surprisingly, the ones closest in usage to the formal-logical *if–then* structure; they express our understanding of our logical reasoning processes, and hence reflect to some extent the same structures inherent in a more formal-mathematical understanding of logic. But they too differ quite clearly from purely formal-logical *if–then* structures: suitable truth-values of antecedent and consequent, although necessary, do not suffice to ensure the felicitousness of an epistemic conditional any more than that of a content conditional. Natural-language epistemic conditionals must have some presumed relationship between the two clauses, just as any conjoined clauses in natural language are assumed to be related. If we were to try to give (1) a natural-language epistemic interpretation, we would have to create a significant amount of context relating protasis and apodosis.

(1) If Paris is the capital of France, (then) two is an even number.

Here we might imagine Woody Allen assuring himself of his sanity after a prolonged hallucinatory nightmare in which geography and mathematics were equally bizarrely disarranged. The truth of "Paris is the capital of France" assures him that he is in the normal real world rather than still being in the nightmare, and his knowledge that he is in the normal real world allows him to conclude with certainty that mathematics is normal, and hence that two is an even number. This is a complex pragmatic connection between the contents of the two clauses, and is totally unlike the simple truth-value requirements imposed by a logical *if–then*.

5.1.3   Speech-act conditionals

It has been recognized for some time that conditional speech acts exist (see Van der Auwera 1986), and classic examples include cases like (8)–(10):

(8) If I may say so, that's a crazy idea.
(9) If I haven't already asked you to do so, please sign the guest book before you go.
(10) If it's not rude to ask, what made you decide to leave IBM?

In these cases, the performance of the speech act represented in the apodosis is conditional on the fulfillment of the state described in the protasis (the state in the protasis *enables* or *causes* the following speech act). Thus, (8) purports to state an opinion only conditionally on the hearer's permission; (9) purports to make a request *if* that request has not already been made; (10) purports to ask a question *if* it's not rude. The conditions on these speech acts are, not surprisingly, overt statements of the sort of general appropriateness-conditions discussed by Grice (1975) and R. Lakoff (1973). Thus Lakoff's maxims would bar the statement in (8) and the question in (10) if they forced the hearer into an optionless acceptance of an opinion or an optionless need to answer a question (one of her proposed maxims is "Leave options").

I have said that these speech acts "purport" to be conditional, since in fact their actual pragmatic status is somewhat nebulous. The sort of politeness conditions stated in (8) and (10) don't in fact prevent (8) from actually stating, or (10) from actually asking a question. Given that the apodosis is actually *present* in such speech acts, the conditional speech act is in some sense always accomplished – at least in the sense that the utterance expressing that speech act is produced. However, (9) might be read as "For the purposes of our interaction, we'll *consider* that I make the following request *if* I didn't previously make it." Although one might say that the request *has* been made, whether it is appropriate or superfluous, we may note that in fact the usual compliance conditions bind the hearer precisely if the request is appropriate. So we may say that the speech act is fully accomplished – in that its illocutionary force actually takes effect – only conditionally. Similarly, in the cases of (8) and (10), the statement is made and the question is asked – but not quite fully. Although it is hard for a hearer to reply overtly, "No, you may *not* say so," or "I'm sorry, it *is* rude to ask that," nonetheless politeness conditionals somehow do allow the hearer a little more room to maneuver. "If I may say so" has perhaps become so idiomatic that it no longer has any genuine conditional value; for most speakers it simply

politeness conditionals not true conditionals but do allow the hearer some option

marks politeness rather than carrying its literal meaning. But in (10), at least, it seems to me that the hearer could more easily reply, "Well, I'd rather not discuss that" than if there had been no conditional attached. In so doing, the hearer would tacitly be taking advantage of the conditional, and thus not assuming the usual responsibility of replying to a question.[5]

The way in which conditional speech acts are actually performed, but present themselves as only conditionally performed, is parallel to the way in which speech-act uses of *or* present two alternative speech acts (while necessarily needing to perform both in order to allow the interlocutor to "choose" between them). Both appear to rely on the interlocutor's cooperation in helping keep some jointly agreed-on mental record of what counts as "really" having been said, and on a convention which puts on that record only one of two alternative speech acts, and which only conditionally records a conditional speech act.

The cases discussed above are generally-accepted examples of conditional speech acts. However, by applying the same analysis to some less obvious examples, we can simplify a number of troublesome cases which have been worrying linguists and philosophers ever since Austin's classic "Ifs and cans" (1961). Let us take as our first instance Austin's example (1961, pp. 210–12):

(11) There are biscuits on the sideboard if you want them.

Austin never fully resolves the difficulties inherent in (11), but observes correctly that in no sense can the actual presence of the biscuits be said to be conditional upon the hearer's desire to eat one. In my opinion, (11) is a conditional speech act parallel to (8)–(10) above – we should read (11) as, "*If* you want biscuits, then (let us consider that) I *inform* you that there are biscuits on the sideboard." Notice that, in a slightly more complex way, this conditional speech act invokes the Gricean maxims just as (8)–(10) invoked them. The act of informing the hearer of the biscuits' presence is only *relevant* in the case of the hearer's being supposed to be hungry for a biscuit. So, even though the speaker did not state a condition expressly invoking relevance or informativeness (such as, "if I haven't already told you"), the condition "if you want them" presents us with the Gricean sufficient condition for making the previous statement – and, equally, for the offer inherent in the statement. A better reading for this example at the speech-act level might in fact be, "I hereby *offer* you some biscuits on the sideboard, *if* you want them." Given this reading, the speech-act status of *if* comes out even more clearly: the offer is conditional on its potential acceptability to the hearer (Searle's felicity condition for an offer [1969]).

An expanded definition of conditional speech acts would thus include all cases where the performance of the in-process speech act (the apodosis) is presented as being conditional on some factor expressed in the protasis. It is my belief that all such cases are inherently Gricean (or Searlean), in that the conditional protases in question invariably refer to some relevance condition or felicity condition of the relevant speech-act category. However, some such speech-act conditionals are overtly Searlean (one might say, overtly metalinguistic) in that they explicitly invoke rules of linguistic interaction (see [8]–[10]) such as, "don't be rude," or "be informative (hence, don't repeat)." Others, such as (11), invoke the same sort of felicity conditions at a lower level, or more implicitly – e.g., "if you want them" is a lower-level instance of "if you want me to make this offer" or "if it will fulfill the appropriate desire in the hearer."

Another example of such an implicit invocation of general felicity conditions may be seen in (12):

(12) If you went to the party, was John there?

Let us set aside for the moment a reading which asks whether, for all past "goings to the party," corresponding events of John's presence there occurred.[6] The other reading of (12) is a conditional question, which may be interpreted as, "*If* you went to the party, *then* consider that *I ask you* whether John was there." For a question to be felicitous (Searle 1969), the hearer must be presumed to potentially know the answer. And in fact the only reasonable understanding of this speech-act-conditional reading of (12) is one in which the hearer's going to the party is the condition which enables him or her to have the relevant knowledge. Thus, a higher-level paraphrase might be, "If you *do* know the answer, then take me as asking this question seriously."

An allied but not identical case of implicit Searlean conditionality is (13):

(13) If you went to the party, did you see John?

Now, (13) may be used as a less direct way of asking (12). But it may also be the case that the speaker is actually interested in whether the addressee has managed to see John, rather than in John's presence at the party, but the speaker also knows that the only likely place for the addressee to have seen John lately was at the party. In this case, the question "Did you see John?" is presented as being asked conditionally on the addressee's having gone to the party, *not* because the past party-going would enable the hearer to answer the question, but rather because the past party-going would make the question *relevant*. Questions are only felicitous when the speaker does not already know the answer. If the hearer didn't go to the party, then the speaker already knows the answer – hence the question is unnecessary.

It thus becomes clear that there are a great variety of conditional speech acts, some more overtly referring to the general felicity conditions on the relevant class of speech acts, while others refer implicitly to these general conditions by referring overtly to some more specific felicity condition on the particular utterance (a sub-case of the general condition). All speech-act conditionals have in common the fact that they are appropriately paraphrased by "If [protasis], then let us consider that I perform this speech act (i.e., the one represented as the apodosis)." This reading is to be contrasted with both content conditionals (which do not need paraphrases involving speech acts or logical processes) and with epistemic conditionals, which are appropriately paraphrased as "If *I know* [protasis], then *I conclude* [apodosis]."[7]

5.2   Real and apparent ambiguities between classes of conditionals

5.2.1   *Comrie's "bicausal" conditionals*
Comrie (1986) discusses examples parallel to (11), in particular (14):

(11) There are biscuits on the sideboard if you want them.
(14) If it will amuse you, I will tell you a joke.

Comrie's interest in examples like (14) is that such cases are ostensibly counter to the normal direction of causality and conditionality. Real-world causality would normally be thought of as involving the joke as cause of the amusement, whence one might rather expect to find conditionals like (15):

(15) If I tell you a joke, it will amuse you.

But in (14) the potential resulting amusement is the cause of the joke's being proffered (*motivation*, rather than cause in any deterministic sense) – and will presumably also be the cause of the joke's being told, if that occurs.

Comrie recognizes that (14) must be understood as a speech-act conditional, although he does not give it a detailed analysis. However, he (mistakenly, in my view) refers to (14) as "bicausal," in that the conditionality of the *if* seemingly operates in both directions: from joke-telling to amusement and from amusement to joke-telling. I see it as crucial to distinguish between speech-act conditionality and content conditionality in these cases: the former is involved in (14) and the latter in (15), but Comrie evidently wants to see both as copresent in (14).

In order to show that (14) is not really "bicausal" – i.e., that the conditional form of (14) marks only speech-act conditionality (whatever other causal and conditional relationships may be pragmatically present) – let us compare (14) and (11). So far as I can tell, the *if* of (14) is precisely parallel to the *if* of (11); both reflect the purported presentation of a speech act (an offer, in both cases) as conditional on the addressee's potential receptiveness. The major felicity condition for an offer is (as mentioned above) that the speaker assumes the hearer to want the thing offered. An offer is therefore infelicitous (or even irrelevant, in Gricean terms) if it fails in fact to respond to a desire or need on the part of the addressee. At an informational level, the statement "There are biscuits on the sideboard" is only a *usefully* informative act if it provides information which the hearer's current situation makes relevant. The indirect offer accomplished via this statement is likewise only felicitous if the addressee is potentially receptive to it. The same is true of the offer to tell a joke in (14): the addressee's potential readiness to be amused by the joke renders the offer felicitous. Thus far I can see no difference between the conditional structures of (11) and (14). Both are essentially "I hereby offer X, if X is a felicitous offer," which is a normal conditional speech-act structure.

What about the fact that in (14) the joke will supposedly cause the amusement at the content level, as well as the intended amusement causing the offer of the joke at the speech-act level? Certainly there is no parallel to this problem in (11): there is no necessary intimation in (11) that the biscuits' presence is a condition or a cause for the addressee's wanting them (although such might be the case, in fact). And my claim is that no such content-level conditionality is linguistically represented in (14), either: it is simply a fact that (15) and (14) may both be true. There is a general motivation behind such a relationship, namely our understanding that if X causes Y (or Y is conditional upon X), then our desire for Y may make us desire X in order to get Y. Thus, from a pragmatic viewpoint, the *truth* of the content conditional in (15) – the fact that in the real world a joke will presumably cause amusement – may be intimately connected with the *felicitousness* of the speech-act conditional in (14). I make my *offer* of joke-telling conditional on potential resulting amusement precisely because I know that amusement may be conditioned by joke-telling in the real world. But this is not to say that both conditions are *linguistically* represented in (14). In fact, (14) seems precisely parallel to (11) in linguistic structure – it is at the pragmatic level that we feel (14) to be different and to be linked to (15).

5.2.2   *Epistemic versus content versus speech act*

Comrie also conflates epistemic and speech-act conditionals (as does all work in the area to date), and this may be the moment to examine some of the ways in which uses of conditionals in the three domains can appear indistinct from each other. Take, for example, the content-domain conditional in (16):

(16) If he's already gone, (then) they will have to leave a message.

The most natural reading of (16) is one wherein "his" absence is a sufficient condition for "their" leaving a message, in the real world. There is a potential link of causation between the two events in the real world. This link might, at first glance, seem to be reversed in a case like (17):

(17) If they have to leave a message, (then) he's gone already. *≠ epistemic-making, the conclusion he is gone*

Here it seems that the message-leaving is a condition for the absence. But this is an illusion. Example (17) is an epistemic conditional, which may be understood as meaning "If I know that they have to leave a message, then I conclude that he's gone already." The reversal of protasis content and apodosis content between (16) and (17) is a result of the fact that (as previously remarked in section 4.1.1) we often *reason* from effect to cause, as well as from cause to effect. Likewise, if event or state X is conditional on the existence of event or state Y, then (supposing the conditionality to be a strong iff conditionality, as in [16]) our *conclusion* that Y is in effect may be conditional on knowing X to be in effect. We may, under appropriate conditions, reason from apodosis to protasis, as well as from protasis to apodosis. *presuppose* *reflected in the conditional structure*

Individual sentences may even be ambiguous between content and epistemic-conditional readings, e.g. (18):

(18) If he was already gone, (then) they had to leave a message.

One reading of (18) is a content-domain conditional reading, which might be paraphrased as "Whenever, in the past, he was gone before their arrival, they were (thereby?) obliged to leave a message." The other is an epistemic reading, which might be paraphrased as: "If I know that he was gone before they arrived (in this instance), then I conclude that they were obliged to leave a message." Notice that (as with modals) verb tenses help sway interpretation from epistemic to content or vice versa: the future tense in (16)'s apodosis helps make a content reading likely, although not inevitable.

Continuing to the speech-act domain, I have already remarked that Comrie's "bicausal" conditionals appear to reverse the usual direction of causality and conditionality. I argue that this apparent reversal is an artifact, and disappears in the face of a clear distinction between content-domain conditionality and speech-act-domain conditionality. If a speaker hopes that her or his speech act will have some real-world result (a result which will be conditional upon the performance of the speech act, in the content domain), then (s)he may (in the speech-act domain) *present* the performance of the act as conditional upon its having that result. But these are two distinct relationships, and only the latter relationship is marked in the linguistic form, in the case just described.

Finally, most previous work has shared one other major conflation of categories: like epistemic causal conjunction (see Ross 1970; Davison 1973), epistemic conditionals have been understood as cases of speech-act conjunction. Thus Comrie presents as speech-act conditionals both cases like (19) and cases like (20):

(19a) If you're so smart, what's the ten-word summary of Wittgenstein's thought?
(19b) If it will satisfy you to know it, Mary is already on her way here.
(20)   If he believes in reincarnation, he's too crazy to bother about.

The cases in (19) are what I refer to as speech-act conditionals – the protasis is a supposed condition for the performance of the speech act in the apodosis. The speaker of (19b) purports to be reluctant to tell the addressee of Mary's impending arrival, but states it conditionally on its having the result of satisfying the addressee's concern. Example (20), on the other hand, does not purport to be a conditionally performed illocutionary act. Rather, the protasis expresses the sufficient condition for the speaker's *concluding the truth* of the apodosis. Example (20) is therefore an epistemic conditional.

Despite ambiguous sentences which may be read as conditionals in more than one domain, the three separate domains and their three uses of *if–then* conditionals remain distinct from one another. Conditionality exists in the content, epistemic, and speech-act domains, just as causal conjunction and other varieties of conjunction are manifested in all three of these domains. A given example may be *ambiguous* between interpretations in two different domains, as in (18), but no *one* interpretation of an *if–then* sentence (such as the most reasonable reading of Comrie's [14]) simultaneously expresses conditionality in more than one domain.

different interpretations may occupy different domains but never simultaneously

5.3   *If* as a topic marker

Haiman (1978), remarking that various unrelated languages show identity or morphological relatedness between the topic marker and the protasis marker, argues convincingly that this apparently odd formal convergence is due to a close affinity between the two categories. The crucial characteristic of a conditional, says Haiman, is that the protasis forms a background against which a comment is proffered. This claim, of course, is revolutionary inasmuch as it explicitly formulates a prototype for conditionals which has nothing to do with formal-logical conditionality. What conditionals have in common, according to Haiman, is not a logical structure but an informational structure. Or, perhaps more precisely, a conditional protasis is to logical informational structure what a topic is to a more general kind of informational structure: the groundwork for some forthcoming addition to the scene.[8]

Although Haiman's claims have some truth behind them – the formal correlation between topic markers and protasis markers is a point not to be ignored – it nonetheless seems to me that conditionals are more complex in meaning than Haiman suggests. Among the issues to be considered are: (a) the degree and nature of the identification between protases and topics: given that there is sufficient similarity between the two categories for them to be sometimes identically marked, what does that tell us? What about various other supposed characteristics of linguistic conditionals: hypotheticality of the protasis, or the (nebulous) link between conditionality and causality? (b) If Haiman's Hua conditionals really are "topics," does this mean the same is true of English conditionals? Haiman himself states that different languages demarcate the conditional category differently. Hua does not mark as "conditional" the semantic equivalents of English counterfactual conditionals, while English grammarians (see Jespersen 1940, 1964, for example) have generally considered atypical the "given that X" sense of *if*-clauses which

different languages mark conditionals differently

is typical in Hua. Haiman feels the *prototype* for "conditional" is nonetheless the same crosslinguistically, and hence the English and Hua categories should be identified with each other.

I think these questions can profitably be examined in the light of the analysis I have just presented. Conditionality "means" different things in different domains, and the degree of convergence between conditionality and topicality needs to be understood against the background of the basic content/epistemic/speech-act ambiguity.

5.3.1   Protases as "given" information or as sufficient conditions?

If conditional protases are to be understood as topics (in the sense of "given information"), then the words "topic" and "given" must undergo a certain amount of redefinition. I set aside the much-discussed issue of whether givenness can be taken as the primary attribute of a topic, a view which Haiman (1978) supports. Whether the topic is *old* information (given as opposed to new) or mentally *present* information (what is talked about), an English counterfactual protasis can hardly be said to be a traditionally defined topic. In order to make a counterfactual protasis a topic, we must assume that a topic is any linguistic unit which expresses a background relative to which something else is presented. Such a background need not be "given" in the sense of already being accepted as certain in the minds of speaker and addressee. A protasis is, rather, "given" in the sense that its acceptance (even if hypothetical) must presumably precede any consideration of the contents of the apodosis: it is given *only relative to the apodosis*.

However, even supposing we accept that a protasis is given or topical, does this observation define conditionality? Surely not. Many other linguistic structures present one thing as a background against which something else is dependently presented. For example, *since*-clauses could be said to have this function, and so could *given that* and *assuming that* as conjunctions. Compare the examples below:

(21) Well, *if* (as you say) he had lasagne for lunch, he won't want spaghetti for dinner.

(22) Well, *since* he had lasagne for lunch, he won't want spaghetti for dinner.

(23) Well, $\left\{ \begin{array}{l} assuming\ that \\ given\ that \end{array} \right\}$ he had lasagne for lunch, he won't want spaghetti for dinner.

Examples (21)–(23) are similar in structure: in each case, the first clause forms the basis for supposing the truth of the second clause. But there are crucial differences as well. *Since* expresses a more overt causal link between the two clauses than any of others, and also presupposes the truth of its complement. *Given that* also tends towards presupposition of the complement, while *assuming that* and *if* do not presuppose anything; if anything, the *given-that* example might be taken as more traditionally topical than the *if* example. But we are missing the point if we fail to notice that the *conditionality* expressed by *if* (as opposed to the causality expressed by *since,* or the presupposition of *given that*) is in itself a semantic component independent of the given–new information dimension. Although conditional protases may frequently present given information, they have other more specific functions, and topicality is not a definition of conditionality.

Returning to my earlier definition, the idea of conditional protases as *sufficient conditions* for the fulfillment of the apodosis would certainly elucidate the link between conditionality and causality, and also the hypothetical status of conditionals. Von Wright (1975) neatly captures the inherently causal nature of conditionals when he argues that our human capacity for deliberately intervening in events (thus changing their default course) is at the root of our understanding of both conditionality and causality: the idea of a *possible* causal intervention is the essence of conditionality. If von Wright is correct, the frequent (although not invariable) hypothetical nature of conditional protases would fit in well with his scheme; as has often been suggested, the protasis would be the introduction to a hypothetical world, resembling the real world except in the one change caused by the possible intervention. The causal intervention in question (whether human and agentive, or not) is presumably to be seen as sufficient to enable or bring about the truth of the apodosis. Such a view seems coherent with our previous observation that conditionality has meaning above and beyond topicality.

Can a sufficient-condition definition of conditionality be reconciled with the observation that conditionals (like various other linguistic structures) frequently show a correlation with topicality? Can we even perhaps *explain* the correlation between protases and topics on the basis of this earlier definition? If we could manage to do this, we would simultaneously define conditionality in such a way as to distinguish the semantics of (21) from that of (22) and (23), and yet also be able to take into account Haiman's observed correlations.

5.3.2   *"Given conditionals" in English: why and when protases are topical*

So-called "given conditionals" (conditionals with "presupposed" protasis content) are among the crucial points in Haiman's argument for identifying conditionality and topicality. As previously remarked, "given" conditionals have often been treated as atypical by English grammarians, but are central members of the class of conditionals in the Papuan language Hua, and may also be common in other languages. Before treating the question of identity between conditionals in different languages, let us examine the class of English conditionals where the protasis is indisputably given information, to see why and how conditionality and topicality cooccur in these cases.

The first thing to note is that (as far as I have been able to discern) English "given" conditionals are all epistemic or speech-act conditionals.[9] I will later attempt to explain why this should be so; for the moment suffice it to say that content-domain conditionals always remain at least somewhat hypothetical. Thus, typical epistemic examples of "given" protases in English include (21) and (24) (the parenthetical expressions are intended to force a "given" protasis reading):

(21) Well, if (as you say) he had lasagne for lunch, he won't want spaghetti for dinner.

(24) If (as they just announced) they're looking for an apartment, they're planning a wedding before long.

Examples (21) and (24) are ordinary epistemic conditionals: in each case, the structure is "If I *know* that X is true, then I *conclude* that Y." (Knowing X is a sufficient condition for concluding Y.) In (21) we can contrast the "given" epistemic reading (the reading that we might loosely paraphrase by replacing *if* with the complement-presupposing *since*) with a content-domain reading wherein the protasis is not given. Remove the parenthesized portion of (21), and there is a content-conditional reading wherein the real-world refusal to eat spaghetti is conditional upon a previous real-world eating of lasagne (X happening is a sufficient condition for Y happening). But, in contrast with the epistemic-conditional reading, the lasagne-eating cannot be taken as a *given*; rather, we must assume that it is still hypothetical (the speaker is uncertain whether in fact the subject ate lasagne for lunch).

Note that, even for the epistemic reading, the "given" protasis is not rigidly presupposed. We can continue (21) with "but I don't believe he had lasagne for lunch." The "givenness" which Haiman finds typical of conditionals seems to reside rather in the speech setting than in the conditional semantics proper. One common way of *using* conditionals is to argue from an already-shared belief of speaker and hearer to a not-yet-shared belief.

For (24), a content-conditional reading is not easy to produce. The reason is that (as we have seen in various earlier examples) the speaker is reasoning from effect to cause. *Knowledge* of an apartment hunt may be sufficient condition for a conclusion about wedding plans in the epistemic world; but in the real world it is more reasonably the wedding plans which are the sufficient condition for carrying out the apartment hunt. Example (25), which is appropriately ordered for a content-conditional reading, is ambiguous in exactly the same way as (21):

(25) If they're planning a wedding, they'll be looking for an apartment soon.

Once again, I find it impossible to get a "given" ("as we both know") reading for the protasis under a content-domain conditional interpretation of the whole sentence: the protasis is hypothetical if the conditional is content-domain.

Some examples of "given" speech-act conditionals are seen in (26) and (27) below:

(26) If (as we both know) you were at the party, how's Harry these days?
(27) If you're so smart (as you seem to think), what was the date of Charlemagne's coronation?

Examples (26) and (27), like the epistemic "given" conditionals discussed above, could easily be paraphrased with *since* replacing *if* – the synonymy between the *since* and *if* sentences indicates the presupposed status of the protases in the conditional examples. The structure of (26) and (27) is "If X is the case, then I present myself as carrying out the speech act represented in the apodosis."

(28) If I was a bad carpenter, I was a worse tailor.[10]

Example (28) is a more complex case, but unlike Haiman I cannot read the protasis of (28) as a simple topic. Example (28) does not mean "Given that I was a bad carpenter, I was a worse tailor." My original analysis of it was something like, "(Even) if (I admit that) I was a bad carpenter, (I still insist that) I was a worse tailor." (I will return to the question of "even if" readings of *if* in the next section). One can imagine the sequence continuing to say either "and so I am right to give up on making a living" or "and so I am right to go back to carpentry." That is, the suggestion of quitting tailoring stands in a concessive-conditional relationship to the other suggestion of quitting carpentry. However, although I still think this may be a correct analysis of *some* possible readings of (28), Dancygier (1987, and forthcoming)[11] has convinced me that the most basic reading of (28), and probably the one intended by Defoe, should be analyzed rather as what she calls a *metalinguistic* conditional, reading something like "If the word *bad* is the right word to describe my carpentry, then I'll have to use *worse* to describe my tailoring." That is, the conditional relationship appears to be between two choices of linguistic form in the utterance, rather as the metalinguistic negation in *Those aren't* TOMAYTOES, *those are* TOMAHTOES (see chapter 1) is understood by Horn (1985) as negating a choice of lexical item. I shall discuss metalinguistic conditionals again later in this chapter.

Returning to the question of "given" conditionals in the speech-act domain, let us examine some of the interpretations of (29):

(29) If he was a bad governor, he'll be a worse president. *can say it is hypothetical to get a content reading*

Assuming that speaker and hearer *do* take the protasis of (29) as given, the sentence is interpreted as either a speech-act conditional or an epistemic conditional. The speech-act reading might be paraphrased as, "(Even) if it's true he was a bad governor (so you want to kick him upstairs), nonetheless (I insist that) he will be a worse president (so he'll do more harm there and should remain governor)." (There is also presumably a Dancygier-style metalinguistic reading, which I am setting aside for the moment.) The epistemic reading might be paraphrased as "If, as I/we know, he was a bad governor, then I conclude he will be a worse president." If, however, we assume that the *if*-clause of (29) is hypothetical, then a content reading becomes possible, which might be paraphrased as "(I don't know what sort of a governor he was, but) his being a bad governor is a sufficient condition to enable his becoming a worse president." Once again, we see that a non-given *if*-clause is necessary in order for a conditional to have a content reading.

So it seems that, at least in English, "given" conditional interpretations exist only in the speech-act and epistemic domains. Why should this be so? My answer is (because we have social reasons to present our own speech acts and conclusions as conditional even when we know or strongly believe the precondition to be true, while we normally have equally strong social reasons *not* to present real-world events as conditional unless the precondition really is hypothetical (and the resulting event thus still in doubt).⌋

In a sense, "given" conditionals are unreasonable. "If X, then Y" logically reduces to "Y" when "X" is already one of the basic premises. So it would be more informative just to say "Y," at least *prima facie*. And our *content-level* usage seems to obey the maxim of informativeness. Why, then, doesn't a speaker just say "John won't want a spaghetti dinner," rather than producing the "given" epistemic conditional, "Well, if (as you say) John had lasagne for lunch, he won't want spaghetti for dinner"? Presumably, the answer is that it is often useful to display the train of reasoning leading to the conclusion expressed. The speaker's epistemic world is not available for direct examination by the addressee, and hence the speaker can't refer to it so casually as to the common external world. Besides, the display of a reasoning sequence marks a speech act as expressing an epistemic-domain event. Thus, "John won't want a spaghetti dinner" simply refers to a real-world situation; but a preceding epistemic conditional (like other markers such as "I guess," "I conclude," "I suppose," "probably," or even "so" and "then") marks the fact that an internal act of concluding is being represented, hence we should really understand the apodosis as "(*I conclude that*) John won't want a spaghetti dinner."[12]

A similar argument can be brought forward to explain speech-act "given" conditionals. Like the epistemic world, the speech-act world is an intangible one; although it is shared by speaker and addressee, it is also in the process of constant, bargained revision. It cannot be referred to as casually as the external tangible world, because it is in fact *built up* by the references made to it. Presenting a speech act conditionally ("If you went to the party, how's Harry?") may help to show how the speech acts fits into the structure of the jointly constructed conversational world. "How's Harry?" is relevant conditionally on the addressee's having been at the party, and even if his/her party attendance is already a shared belief of the speaker and hearer, a display of conditional relevance succeeds in giving the question a context. Furthermore, the domain of speech acts is the interactional domain, where politeness takes on a paramount importance. Explaining or justifying a speech act is often crucial to avoiding rudeness. Thus, even if the speaker actually means to unambiguously perform a given speech act, and therefore expresses its performance as contingent only on a "given" protasis, tacking on a condition still makes the speech

speech acts

act politer by presenting justification. The conditional form itself probably also has weight here; whether or not the protasis is actually hypothetical, conditionals *feel* less assertive and certain than their non-conditional counterparts.

It can thus be useful for speakers to present "given" conditionals in the epistemic and speech-act domains, because an epistemic or speech-act conditional serves some purposes which are irrelevant to content-domain conditionals. A content-domain conditional simply states that X is a sufficient condition for Y in the real world. Such information is irrelevant if Y is known to be *true*; hence, if X is already a background presupposition of speaker and hearer, then the speaker would do better to simply say "Y" rather than "If X, then Y." But for epistemic and speech-act conditionals, the conditional structure may be relevant even when the content of the protasis is already accepted by both interlocutors. In these cases, the protasis does indeed serve the purposes of a sentence topic, in that it presents background for the apodosis or picks out the context in which the apodosis is to be viewed.

5.3.3   Topicality and the universal conditional category

The presentation of topics, or of given information, is a function served by a large number of different linguistic structures. In the preceding section I have tried to explain why givenness should be a normal functional concomitant of semantically hypothetical conditional structures, under certain circumstances. It is thus possible to derive an understanding of "given" conditionals' topicality from a *functional* analysis of conditionals which presumes their basic *semantic* content to be that of sufficient conditionality. I cannot see how, conversely, a sufficient-conditional reading of *if* would follow from its being basically (semantically) a topic marker. So it seems reasonable to suggest that the topicality of *if*-clauses is essentially a pragmatic phenomenon, although it is a normal pragmatic extension of the sufficient-condition definition of *if*.

It remains unclear to me how much of my analysis is applicable to conditionals as a universal category. English conditional protases do not seem best analyzed as clausal topics pure and simple. In trying to decide whether conditionals are prototypically topics in universal grammar, there are still a large number of unanswered questions. For example, many non-conditional subordinate clauses tend in different ways either to present "presupposed" or "given" content, or to present material serving as background to the content of the main clause; this is particularly true of subordinate clauses which precede the main clause. In órder to prove that conditionals are *especially* topical, it would be necessary to show that there is no similar correlation between topic markers and other classes of subordinating conjunctions (e.g. causals). It would also be useful to examine correlations between word order (protasis–apodosis is "normal" universally, but many languages also allow apodosis–protasis; in English and French neither order seems especially marked) and topicality of the protasis (or identity of protasis marker and topic marker). And, of course, languages such as Hua might be reexamined to see whether the analysis I have given can be extended beyond English.

I thus leave open the question of universal identity between prototypical conditionals and clausal topics. Haiman's explanation for the correlation between the two categories is reasonable, but is also perfectly coherent with (a) a more traditional sufficient-condition semantics of conditional sentences, and (b) similar functional correlations between topicality and other (non-conditional) kinds of subordinate clauses. Furthermore, in English at least, the *most* topical conditionals ("given" conditionals) can be shown to be special functional extensions of conditionality to the needs of the epistemic and speech-act domains.

5.4   The *even-if* reading of conditionals

5.4.1   *Relating* if *to* even if

Perhaps the biggest problems for a sufficient-conditionality analysis of *if* are the "if-and-only-if" and "even-if" readings which can be attributed to simple *if*-protases. I have discussed above (section 5.1.1) the way in which an "if-and-only-if" interpretation often follows conversationally from the expression of sufficient conditionality. But how can sufficient conditionality explain the concessive readings of *if*? It would be particularly useful to explain this reading, because if concessive *if* remains unexplained, then *even if* (necessarily concessive) must be analyzed as a different conjunction, unrelated to *if*. Such an analysis would surely be counterintuitive enough to worry most linguists.

Van der Auwera (1986) points out that interrogative conditionals in particular tend to favor an *even-if* reading, so that examples such as (30) are readily capable of bearing either a "normal" or a concessive reading. (Note that [30] is not a conditionally performed question, but a questioned conditional – a question about the conditional "If John comes, you will go.")

(30) If John comes, will you go?

Example (30) can be interpreted either as meaning "Is John's coming a sufficient condition for your going?", or as meaning "Is John's coming a sufficient condition to prevent your going – even if John comes, will you go?" Van der Auwera suggests that the reason why questions readily allow an *even-if* reading is that they inherently bring up both the affirmation and the denial of the questioned proposition. Hence, in (30) the protasis can be taken as a condition either for the truth of the apodosis or for its falsity. Pragmatic considerations will determine which reading prevails in a given situation – if the speaker knows that the addressee hates John, then the normal reading is likely to be in effect, whereas if the addressee is known to be eager to see John, the concessive reading will probably seem reasonable. Compare the following two examples:

(31) Will you go hiking tomorrow if it rains?
(32) Will you go hiking tomorrow if the weather is sunny?

Given our knowledge about likely causal relationships in the real world, we tend strongly toward a concessive interpretation of (31) and a normal interpretation of (32).

Van der Auwera assumes that questioned conditionals are alone in their openness to a concessive interpretation. Haiman (1986) notes, however, that simple assertions can evoke the same two possible interpretations. Thus, (33) (example from Haiman 1986) tends to have a concessive interpretation, while the positive (34) tends to have a normal conditional reading:

(33) I wouldn't marry you if you were the last man on earth.
(34) I would marry you if you were the last man on earth.

But (35), where the pragmatic expectations are reversed from (33), has a "normal" reading as its preferred interpretation, while (36) tends to receive a concessive reading:

(35) I wouldn't marry you if you were a monster from Mars.
(36) I would marry you if you were a monster from Mars.

Haiman states that in English, such concessive *if*-clauses tend to preferentially follow their apodoses; he cites examples such as (33) and (37):

(37) I'll get him if it's the last thing I do.

He further notes that concessive *if*-clauses seem freed from this ordering restraint if they are given a particular intonation pattern: a "contemptuous squeal", including strong stress and high pitch on the final portion of the concessive clause, followed by an abrupt pitch-drop in the apodosis. The "squeal" intonation *avoids* backgrounding of the initial clause; high volume and contemptuous tone make it simultaneously emphasized and dubitative. This same intonation pattern will also allow coordinate *and*-conjuncts to be interpreted concessively – i.e., to be given an "and yet" reading, rather than an "and so" reading. Thus, of the examples below (from Haiman), (38) and (39) are a normal coordinate and a normal conditional, while (40) and (41) are concessive and hence require "squeal" intonation:

(38) You major in math or physics, and CDC will want to hire you.
(39) If you major in math or physics, CDC will want to hire you.
(40) You major in math or THEOLOGY, and CDC will want to hire you.
(41) If you major in math or THEOLOGY, CDC will want to hire you.

Haiman suggests that the reason for the ordering restriction is that the sequence of conjuncts tends to reflect temporal and causal sequence in the real world (see above, chapter 4, on conjunction). The preferred apodosis–protasis order for concessive conditionals presumably follows from the fact that protasis–apodosis order would tend to reinforce a sufficient-condition reading. Thus, to prevent a sufficient-condition reading in (40), or an "and so" reading in (41), a "squeal" intonation is necessary.

Given Haiman's observations, Van der Auwera's explanation seems insufficient; in examples like (33) and (41), the "even-if" interpretation, does not stem from an interrogative form which evokes both affirmation and denial of the apodosis content. It may be the case that interrogatives are particularly susceptible to an "even-if" reading, for the reasons Van der Auwera proposes; but whatever it is that allows "even-if" interpretations of Haiman's examples (33) and (41), the same explanation will account for the "even-if" reading in (31) or the possibility of such a reading in (30).

It seems, then, that while *if*-conditionals are not basically concessive, their semantics has inherent potential for a pragmatically-conditioned concessive reading. Haiman would say that protases, as clausal topics,[13] are background to the apodosis and tend to precede it; hence they tend to be taken as causal precursors to the apodosis, given the effects of word-order iconicity. But the iconic "and-so" interpretation of *and*-conjuncts is not a necessary one, and evidently the "normal" conditional reading is not necessary either – it can be replaced by a concessive reading in the right context, just as *and* can be interpreted as "and yet" in the right context. Haiman's interpretation is tempting, but I still feel reluctant to adopt it. As stated above, it is hard to see what makes conditionals *more* topical than other related varieties of subordinate clauses; and it is easy to see how a sufficient-conditional semantics of *if* could explain conditionality's links with causality on the one hand, and with topicality on the other. How can such an interpretation explain concessive *if*? As we shall see below, the meaning of concessive *if* turns out to be better motivated by a sufficient-condition analysis of *if* than by a topicality analysis.

Concessive *if*-clauses such as (42) are at least close to synonymous with their *even-if* counterparts:

(42) I'll climb that mountain *if* it kills me.
(43) I'll climb that mountain *even if* it kills me.

Now, these examples are certainly concessive in meaning, in that they show one clause in a "despite" relationship with the other: the idea that climbing the mountain will kill me would certainly not be the most natural conjunct for "I'll climb that mountain." But (42) and (43) (and all other examples of *even if* and concessive *if*) are more than simply concessive: they express not only opposition between the two clauses, but the further idea that the protasis represents a relatively *extreme* possibility from among the possible conditions which can be expected to occur in opposition to the truth or the fulfillment of the apodosis. There is an inherent feeling of *scale* involved (in the sense of Fauconnier's [1975] definition of a pragmatic scale).[14]

How such a scalar reading of *if* could be derived from the idea of *if* as a topic marker, I do not know. But it is relatively simply derivable from a sufficient-condition analysis of conditional semantics. If conditionals mean "X is a sufficient condition for Y," then clearly any better situation than X – any situation *more* favorable to Y than X is – will also be sufficient for Y. Suppose I say that certain extremely unfavorable circumstances will nonetheless be sufficiently favorable to ensure Y (or insufficiently unfavorable to allow ~Y). I have produced a very strong statement that Y will occur whatever happens; since nearly all other circumstances are more favorable to Y than X is, Y will almost surely occur. Such, I claim, is the correct interpretation of *even-if* sentences and concessive-*if* sentences.

Only pragmatic context can determine the choice between a normal and a concessive *if*-reading, since it is a pragmatic question whether the set of circumstances expressed in a given protasis are favorable or unfavorable to a given apodosis. Thus, if we can imagine a speaker who has been waiting all his/her life to find and marry a Martian monster, then (35) could reasonably receive a concessive reading, while (36) could be interpreted as a normal conditional:

(35) I wouldn't marry you if you were a monster from Mars.
(36) I would marry you if you were a monster from Mars.

A "concessive" interpretation of the sufficient-conditional *if* is, then, natural under certain circumstances. *Even* simply forces such a reading, so that *even if* is always concessive. This is because *even* is an explicitly scalar expression: if we say "Even Mary likes John," then we presuppose a scale wherein Mary ranks high with respect to a probable tendency not to like John (or low with respect to tendency to like him). Since the concessiveness of a conditional results from the presence of such a scalar context (whether implicit or explicit), *even if* thus appears to be a fairly regular compositional joining of *even* (the explicit marker of scalar context) and *if*. Haiman's "contemptuous squeal," marking concessive meaning, can now perhaps be reinterpreted as the emphasis and tonal rise which mark the presentation of an assertion which is perceived as extreme, or end of scale, in some way. Note that the same tonal pattern occurs with non-conditional sentences such as "Even MARY likes John"; the high-on-scale element, *Mary*, receives stress and high pitch, which mark it as the surprising or extreme element in the sentence.

My conclusion, then, is that the "even-if" reading of conditionals is a pragmatically motivated extension of the basic sufficient-condition semantics of *if*. Although this concessive reading seems somewhat more restricted in application than the basic *if*, it extends beyond the content domain of conditionality, as I shall demonstrate in the following section.

5.4.2 Concessive conditionals in different domains

Although concessive conditionals are less common than normal conditionals, they too can be found in the epistemic and speech-act domains, as well as in the content domain. Earlier in this chapter, in examining Jesperson's example (28), I suggested that one way of looking at it was to see a concessive-conditional relationship between the speech-act forces of the two, protasis and apodosis.

dreaming children

(28) If I was a bad carpenter, I was a worse tailor.

For example, "I am a bad carpenter" might indirectly convey "maybe I should give up on carpentry," while "I am a worse tailor" might therefore convey the opposed "maybe I should go back to carpentry despite how bad I am at it." In this case, the concessive force has effect in the speech-act domain.

Other examples of concessive speech-act conditionals include:

(44) That was a great dinner, if I do say so myself.
(45) (Even) if there are *ten* beers in the fridge, we gotta work.
(46) (Even) if he *is* a stuffed shirt, he's not a fool.

Examples (44)–(46) all have the structure "I say (insist) that X, even if I admit that Y." Example (44) is perhaps particularly interesting: its conveyed meaning is something like "I insist on saying that it was a great dinner, even if I recognize that it's rude for me to praise my own cooking." The speaker must be appealing to some mitigating force in order to allow this boastfulness – the mitigating force being presumably the easily recognizable *truth* of the apodosis.

I suspect that (47)–(49) are also concessive speech-act conditionals:

(47) He's friendly enough, (even) if (he's) a bit patronizing.
(48) She responded enthusiastically, if belatedly.
(49) He's a novelist, if a minor one.

The odd thing about (47)–(49) is that the "sentence fragments" in the protases cannot be replaced by full clauses when the conjunction is simple *if*. Thus, I cannot say (50), although (51) is good:

(50) *He's a novelist, if he's a minor one.
(51) He's a novelist, even if he's (only) a minor one.

A similar contrast can be observed in (52) and (53):

(52) *She responded enthusiastically, if she responded belatedly. (*on a concessive reading)
(53) She responded enthusiastically, even if she (only) responded belatedly.

I am not sure why it should be necessary to spell out *even if* in (51) and (53), but not in (47)–(49). But all of these sentences appear to have the same speech-act structure as (44)–(46): "I assert/insist that X, even if I admit that Y." There is no reason, for example, why (49)–(51) should be concessive at the content or epistemic level; someone's being a novelist is not in any apparent conflict with the same person's being a minor novelist, either in the real world or in the speaker's belief system. Rather, it is the speaker's conversational purposes which are at odds: the speaker may be admitting that the subject (as a minor novelist) is not a major literary figure, but insisting that, nonetheless (as a *bona fide* novelist), the subject is to be taken seriously as a writer.

Epistemic concessive conditionals are much less easy to exemplify than their content-domain and speech-act-domain counterparts. This may be partly due to pragmatic factors. It seems more normal, in stating a conclusion, to say what that conclusion *is* conditional upon than what it *isn't* conditional upon. And, more importantly, epistemic "given" conditionals are extremely common; it is hard to interpret an epistemic conditional with a presupposed protasis as anything but a normal epistemic "given" conditional. But with the right context, a concessive reading becomes possible, at least with the explicitly concessive *even if*:

(54) (seeing the light in the apartment): (So) he's home, even if the paper wasn't picked up this morning.

Example (54) presumably means "I conclude that he's home (from seeing the light), even if I might have thought otherwise from the neglected newspaper on the porch." The crucial factor is that the conclusion has to come from some train of reasoning; since it does not come from the premise expressed in the *even if* clause, it must come from some *other* train of reasoning, which is opposed to that expressed in the protasis. I have been unable to find similar concessive examples which sound natural with *if* rather than with *even if*, although such cases may exist.

Speech-act concessive conditionals show interesting semantic parallels with the speech-act modal uses cited at the end of chapter 3. Thus, (44)–(46) are quite close in meaning to (55)–(57) (see Ransom 1977):

(44) That was a great dinner, *if* I do say so myself.
(45) (Even) *if* there are *ten* beers in the fridge, we gotta work.
(46) *If* he is a stuffed shirt, he's not a fool.
(55) I *may* be the wrong person to say so, *but* that was a great dinner.
(56) There *may* be ten beers in the fridge, *but* we gotta work.
(57) He *may* be a stuffed shirt, *but* he's not a fool.

We could also rephrase sentences like (47) in a similar fashion:

(47) He's friendly enough, *if a* bit patronizing.
(58) He *may* be a bit patronizing, *but* he's friendly enough.

The *if*-sentences above are most naturally interpreted as suggested earlier:

"(I insist that) X, (even) *if* (I admit that) Y." The *may* sentences have the reading. "I *allow* X (into our conversational world), but (I insist) that Y." Conditionality and modality (long known to be related phenomena) can thus be seen to converge in yet one more way, in the speech-act domain as well as in the other domains of language use. Not surprisingly, since concessive use of *may* and *can* appears to be the commonest speech-act use of modality, it is concessive *(even)-if* speech-act conditionals which turn out to find a parallel in the realm of speech-act modality.

5.4.3   Metalinguistic conditionals

I would like to finally touch briefly on Dancygier's (forthcoming) claim that conditionals have a separate metalinguistic use. In chapter 1, I mentioned Horn's (1985) discussion of the many different ways in which negation can be interpreted as commenting on the choice of linguistic form, rather than negating content. In (59)–(61), some of these are exemplified.

(59) That's not a *tomayto*, that's a *tomahto*.
(60) Suzie dear, Fido didn't *pee* on the carpet, he *made a mistake*.
(61) She's not *happy*, she's *ecstatic*.

In each case, the negation denies the correctness of the choice of a particular form; it may be on phonological grounds (as in [59]), registral grounds (as in [60]), or just on the grounds of insufficient semantic accuracy (as in [61]). Horn uses *assertability* to describe what is negated in these cases: that is, in each case, the negation marks the clause in which it appears as unassertable. Given the broad range of phenomena here represented, it may be questioned whether a single term like *assertability* is the best way to describe what they share, but I would agree that the uses are all metalinguistic.

Dancygier argues that conditionals like (62)–(64) should be analyzed as similarly being metalinguistic, in that some aspect of linguistic form is presented conditionally.

(62) Grandma is "feeling lousy," if you'll allow me to put it that way.
(63) OK, I'll have a *tomahto*, if that's how you pronounce it.
(64) John *managed* to solve the problem, if that was at all difficult.

In (62) the speaker uses an expression conditionally on the hearer's acceptance; in (63) the speaker chooses a phonological form based on a premise of accepted pronunciation; in (64) the speaker hedges the use of the word *manage* by making it conditional on the right presuppositions (difficulty, for example) being fulfilled.

Dancygier may well be correct in arguing that these metalinguistic uses of conditionals should be carefully distinguished from standard conditional speech acts. In both cases, the conditional relationship is related to the current speech act's performance, but in these metalinguistic cases, the conditionality does not relate to the force of the speech act itself.

5.5 Conclusions

Conditionality has long been known to be related to causality and modality; Haiman (1986) has argued cogently that it is closely linked with coordinate conjunction as well, although conditional clauses are prototypically subordinate. It is thus no surprise to find that, like causality, modality, and coordination, conditionality too has a multi-faceted existence in the three basic domains of semantic interpretation. This chapter has laid out some of the uses of conditionals in the content, epistemic, and speech-act domains; it has presented evidence for the separation of conditional speech acts from epistemic conditionals, and also for a conditional speech-act analysis of a wider group of utterances than have previously been so categorized.

I have argued that many of Haiman's (1978) parallels between topicality and conditionality can be explained by examining the functional extensions of a sufficient-conditional *if*-semantics into the epistemic and speech-act domains. I have further suggested that the *even-if* reading of conditionals is another natural pragmatic extension of a sufficient-condition interpretation of *if*. Such an analysis may have the added advantage of offering a reasonable explanation for synonymy between speech-act *may* and speech-act concessive *if*. In any case, most of the regularities pointed out in this chapter would remain unobserved or unexplained if conditionality were not analyzed as applying to more than one domain of linguistic usage.

Like *and*, *if* may well have a very abstract meaning, which may be interpreted as applying to either content, epistemic sequence, or speech-act structure. But the kind of causal priority which is evidently important in our interpretation of natural-language conditional sentences has its roots in the content world, and (as has been argued earlier) seems to have been extended from that domain to our understanding of the two more abstract worlds.

Returning to the old and vexed question of resemblance between natural-language conditionals and logical *if–then* (material implication) or other purely truth-conditional analyses of *if–then*, the preceding examination of conditionality would suggest that the linguists and philosophers who have questioned the identity of the two categories were right to do so. (Natural-language conditionals express a relationship and a dependency, not only between the truth values of the two clauses, but between their contents as well.) Von Wright's (1975) interpretation of conditionals as rooted in the idea of possible causal intervention captures this content relationship very effectively (see also Lewis 1975). From the idea of such a dependency between contents, the appropriate pairings of truth values for a logical *if–then* structure will necessarily follow, while the converse is not necessarily so. Natural-language conditionals are more constrained than logical *if–then*.

The analysis of epistemic and speech-act conditionals presents particularly strong evidence for a non-truth-functional, sufficient-conditional analysis of *if–then* sentences in natural language. First of all, the "apodoses" of conditional speech acts often have no truth values, since they can be questions, commands, or requests as easily as assertions. Thus felicity, rather than truth value, must enter into our formal analysis of *if–then*. Secondly, and more importantly, conditional speech acts invariably require an interpretation wherein the protasis expresses a factor which actively influences (causes or enables) the performance of the following speech act. It would be incorrect, as well as insufficient, to simply list possible combinations of truth and felicity conditions, barring the case wherein the protasis is false and the apodosis is felicitous. The protasis' truth constitutes a sufficient condition for the apodosis' felicity because there is a causal link between the two. The same is true for epistemic conditionals: the protasis' truth constitutes a sufficient condition for concluding the truth of the apodosis, because the knowledge of the protasis is taken as causing or enabling the conclusion embodied in the apodosis. An examination of conditionals in areas beyond the content domain thus indicates clearly that (as with other conjunctions) the formal-logical *if–then* derives from the natural-language *if–then*, but the two cannot be identified with each other.

Appendix to section 5.1.3

Van der Auwera (1986) proposes that only "commentative" conditional speech acts (by which term he refers to the overtly Gricean conditionals) are really conditional speech acts. He would group cases similar to (11) (repeated from 5.1.3) with (65) and (66), as "speech acts about conditionals."

(11) There are biscuits on the sideboard if you want them.
(65) If you inherit, will you invest?
(66) If a kangaroo has no tail, it topples over.

Thus (65) is a question about the conditional relationship between inheritance and investment, while (66) is a statement about the conditional relationship between taillessness and toppling over. Van der Auwera admits the existence of a particular class of *indirectly* Gricean conditional *questions* ("Holdcroft questions," after Holdcroft [1971]), which are not questions about conditionals, but real conditional speech-acts, as in the speech-act reading of (67):

(67) If you saw John, did you speak to him?

The speech-act conditional reading of (67) is approximately "If you saw John, then I ask whether you spoke to him." The protasis is indirectly commentative, since "If you saw John" refers to a condition which would enable the answering of the question. But Van der Auwera maintains that such indirect commentative conditional speech acts can only be questions, not assertions or commands. His object is to preserve for a maximal number of cases the principle that the speech-act force is always the highest operator in a formal structure. However, if his reanalysis does not work for questions, it is hard to see what use there is in maintaining it for other speech acts.

Van der Auwera's analysis also does not take into account the existence of indirectly commentative statements, as well as questions; he does not, unfortunately, discuss Austin's "Ifs and cans" example ([11], above), which seems to me an exceptionally clear case. Example (11) cannot be read as an assertion about a conditional relationship between the biscuits' location and the addressee's desires. It is a conditional speech act, and the protasis indirectly refers to the Gricean maxim of relevance; or, if you prefer, it refers to a Searlean condition on an offer, the offer being indirectly expressed by the statement in the apodosis. One can construct examples which are even farther from direct reference to conditions on speech acts, but which nonetheless clearly refer indirectly to such conditions, e.g. (68):

(68) There are biscuits on the sideboard, if you missed lunch.

Missing lunch is a condition which might make one hungry, which in turn might make one want a biscuit, which in turn would make the offer appropriate.

Given cases like (11) and (68), one is forced to view conditional speech acts as extending beyond the *directly* commentative examples. In section 5.1.3, I argued that a Gricean conditional speech-act analysis will account for a much larger class of sentences than has previously been supposed.

Returning to examples such as (65) and (67), I would claim that *both* these examples are ambiguous between a question-about-conditional (content) reading and a conditional-question reading. Example (65) may mean either "Will your investment occur conditionally on your inheritance?" or "Given that you inherit (as we both know), I ask whether you will invest." (See section 5.3 for a discussion of given conditionals.) Example (67) may mean either "Did your speaking to John occur, conditionally on your seeing him (usually, in the past)?" or "If (or given that) you saw John, I ask you whether you spoke to him." Van der Auwera's analysis will not account for this general ambiguity, while my contrast between conditionals in different domains will easily explain such facts.

6   *Retrospect and prospect*

I began this work by offering the reader some examples of apparently puzzling, but common, patterns in historical change of meaning. In the course of chapter 2, certain documented historical trends and synchronic semantic structures were shown to involve a pervasive metaphorical structuring of our internal mental world in terms of our physical world. This structuring is experientially based: our internal self is not objectively "like" our physical self, but our physical and psychological worlds have numerous experiential links drawing them together. Given the concept of structuring one domain in terms of another, the "puzzles" offered at the beginning of chapter 2 were suddenly unmasked as self-evident. No complex unravelling was necessary to explain the link between (for example) *way* and *anyway*, or *grasp* and *understand*; given the structuring of our whole mental vocabulary, these semantic relationships are naturally motivated by the general framework.

A further positive result of this historical analysis is that it is equally applicable to synchronic polysemy-structures. A unified concept of semantic "relatedness," in which one frequent kind of relation is metaphor, can account for both synchronic lexical-meaning structure and diachronic directions in semantic change.

There are two theoretical points which need emphasis here. The first is that one cannot automatically expect a synchronic semantic theory to deal naturally with historical change: I have argued that objectivist feature-analysis is inadequate in this respect. The second is that it may be useful for synchronic semantic analysis itself to examine synchrony and diachrony side-by-side. Historical evidence can be a metric for choosing between different synchronic semantic theories. In this particular case, the choice made is an interesting one: the rejection of an entire class of traditional theories in favor of an analysis which admits metaphor into semantic structure. If polysemy structures are data for cognitive science, then so are etymologies.[1]

A synchronic semantic framework which involves the apparatus mentioned above (the idea of domains, and the concept of experientially based metaphorical structuring of one domain in terms of another) turns out to explain other facts of polysemy and usage variation in English. The root–epistemic–speech-act contrast in the semantics of modal verbs apparently reflects the application of modality to three different domains represented by sentences: real-world content; epistemic premises and conclusions; and speech acts. The latter two domains are structured in terms of the basic content (real-world) domain.

Conjunction and conditionals show the same potential as modals for interpretation in three distinct domains. The extremely varied uses of conjunctions such as *and* and *or* fall out readily from a combination of (a) recognition of their multi-domain applications, and (b) other general principles such as word-order iconicity and an understanding of indirect speech-acts. Bloom and Capatides (1987) have given evidence that children acquiring language apply overt markers of causal sequence later to more subjective and epistemic phenomena than to concrete sequences of events. This seems further evidence in favor of treating the content domain as prior, and the epistemic and speech-act domains as secondary, in the area of causality and conditionality as well as in the area of modality.

A large number of questions remain unanswered, and I can only begin to enumerate some of the areas which I regard as targets for future investigation. First, as mentioned in chapter 3, it seems to me important that Fauconnier's (1985) work on mental spaces should be brought to bear on problems of polysemy as well as on problems of reference. The "connectors" which Fauconnier uses to link individuals across domains could be used to explain polysemy, in the following way. First, let us look at a standard reference example: "In the picture, the girl with blue eyes has green eyes." Interpretation of this utterance requires the postulated existence of two mental spaces, a "real world" and a "picture world," and a *connection* between a real (blue-eyed) girl and her (green-eyed) *counterpart* in the picture. The girl can only be identified with her (non-identical) counterpart in the picture because the picture is evidently structured analogously to the real world in certain ways. Now, let us take the example of a polysemous word, *must*. Let us postulate two mental spaces, one being the domain of sociophysical modality, and the other the domain of logical possibility, probability, and necessity. Given that we experientially structure the latter domain (or space) in terms of the former one, it is possible to talk about connections and counterpart relations between entities in the two domains. Logical necessity is the *counterpart*, in the epistemic space, of force or obligation in the space of sociophysical modality.

Metaphor, polysemy, and coreferentiality across mental spaces are quite different phenomena, but each involves giving a common label to two or more distinct entities. Further, in each case, the common label seems to be bestowed because of a perceived counterpart relation between entities in analogously structured domains. The major difference is that with metaphor (and metaphorically based polysemy) one domain is being structured in terms of the other – whereas with general inter-space connector relations the two spaces could have independent structures which just partially coincide (e.g. "the world last year" vs "the world this year"). Fauconnier's theory of mental spaces seems ideally equipped to investigate regular similarities between metaphor and counterpart coreferentiality, insofar as such similarities exist.

Other investigations into the effects of domain structure in language include the work of Kay (1983), who argues convincingly that our metalinguistic world is structured by at least two distinct (and *conflicting*) folk theories of language use; and Ernst (1984), who takes a large set of domain adverbs (e.g., *biologically, linguistically, academically*) and proposes that their multiple uses can be accounted for on the assumption that such adverbs evoke *presupposed domains* of structured meaning. Ernst, like Kay, notes that the same event or entity may fit into a number of different domain-structures, and those events/entities will be differently perceived depending on which domain is the currently relevant one. Rappaport's (1980) work on "detached" and "non-detached" senses of participial forms in Slavic may reflect (at least in part) a distinction between epistemic and content readings; if so, here is another example of differences in grammatical behavior which reflect differences in the domain of a relation between clauses in an utterance.

From the work of all the above researchers, it seems clear that we cannot escape using the general concept of multiple domain-structures in our analysis of linguistic meaning. This study has argued for the necessity of metaphorically structuring domains in terms of each other. And, most crucially, I have presented evidence to suggest that some of the same basic domain-structures can give a consistent and illuminating account of previously puzzling phenomena in the apparently disparate areas of (a) semantic change; (b) polysemy structure; and (c) interpretation of sentence conjunction. Particularly interesting is the idea that the speech-act domain is structured (at least, one of its possible structurings) by the content domain; the concept of speech-act *force* takes on a new dimension if we understand it to be a metaphorical extension of real-world force.

It has for some time been known[2] that grammaticalization is one common result of semantic change towards more abstract meanings; in fact, perhaps the most common historical source of grammatical morphemes is development from a concrete lexical meaning (as *go* has developed a future sense in English *gonna*). We will thus, in elucidating the regularities inherent in semantic change, be exposing new generalizations about the semantic basis for grammar.

A narrowly synchronic view of linguistic structure, or an objectivist view of meaning which failed to deal with metaphor, or even a narrowly linguistic view which failed to take into account our understanding of how we use language, would not be able to explain the synchronic and diachronic patterns of meaning which are treated in this work. My hope is that future work in semantics will move towards the examination of meaning in its larger historical and cognitive setting.

Notes

1   Introduction

1 Later in this chapter I will resume some of the work in question – see section 1.2 for a discussion of linguistic, anthropological, and psychological literature which converges on this viewpoint.

2 Classic polysemy examples include *see* ("visually perceive/mentally understand") and *brilliant* ("giving off a strong light/extremely intelligent"), which will be referred to in chapter 2; also the multiple senses of *bachelor* (see Bolinger 1965). Classic homonymy cases include *bank* ("river bank/financial institution") and *there/their* (frequent spelling confusions confirm the purely conventional nature of the orthographic separation between this pair).

3 Horn's work (see especially Horn 1985) has discussed wider, pragmatic aspects of negation; and in future chapters other authors' work on pragmatic aspects of certain lexical areas will be discussed.

4 Lip service is sometimes paid to the idea that a full lexical-semantic analysis is necessary; but in practice formal semanticists have frequently contented themselves with the use of capital letters as shorthand for an unanalyzed lexical semantics.

5 Bolinger (1977) offers a strong critique of this trend in generative linguistic treatments of lexical meaning.

6 On the other hand, the pun on the two senses of *believe in* in this example is further evidence of the fact that not all belief (or knowledge) concerns visible or tangible events and entities.

7 Sapir's (1921) *Language* and Whorf's (1956b [1941]) essay "The relation of habitual thought and behavior to language" are among the major works arguing for a bidirectional relationship between language and cultural or cognitive structure.

8 There is psychological evidence to support the cognitive reality of metaphorical structuring (for example, Gentner and Gentner 1982). I realize that there are researchers who still seriously question the cognitive reality of metaphor; however, I see the historical linguistic data presented here as a quite inescapable argument. It seems to me impossible to explain metaphorical structuring of regular trends in meaning-change, without admitting the cognitive reality of the structures in question.

9 One important *partial* correlation which presumably underlies these metaphors

is that of daylight with visibility, warmth, and relative safety, while night has the corresponding negative connotations. Since commenting on the relationship between such color metaphors and racism would be the subject of another book, I will forbear to address the subject here.

10 Saussure (1959 [1915], pp. 22–23, 88ff., and 110).

11 It may be that different metalinguistic aspects of the utterance are negated in examples like (a) and (b):

(a)   She's *not* happy, she's ecstatic.
(b)   She's *not* buying tomaytoes, she's buying tomahtoes.

(a) seems to involve negative metalinguistic comment on the speaker's lexical choice, while (b) comments on pronunciation. These two comments are clearly both metalinguistic, but whether *assertability* is the ideal term for what they have in common may be subject to discussion.

12 Among the seminal discussions of the relationship between content and speech-act force are Grice (1975, 1978), Gordon and Lakoff (1971), R. Lakoff (1972b, 1973), and Searle (1969, 1979).

13 The work of Wierzbicka (e.g. 1980) is the only serious attempt in this direction which I have seen, and is subject to the same criticisms as all the smaller-scale attempts, in that there seems little motivation for the choice of included primes and the exclusion of other features from the prime list: the chosen primes often have interest and seem relevant to semantic structure, but one could keep on adding forever.

14 See Sweetser (1987b) for a fuller treatment of these metaphors for thought and speech.

2   **Semantic structure and semantic change: English perception-verbs in an Indo-European context**

1 This chapter draws on my earlier work on English perception-verbs (Sweetser 1984a). In addition to works explicitly cited, the following sources have been used regularly: Chantraine (1968–1980) and Ernout and Meillet (1959).

2 Striking evidence that this viewpoint is still in force is found in Hock (1986), whose chapter on semantic change does treat some work on general directions in meaning-change, but does not mention the recent work of Traugott, for example. The chapter concludes that "under certain circumstances semantic change can be quite regular and systematic. However, this should not detract from the fact that in most cases, semantic change is 'fuzzy,' highly irregular, and extremely difficult to predict" (p. 308).

3 As Meillet so wisely observed (Meillet 1937 [1984], p. 382), "Relating words from different languages requires us to concentrate on their common denominator, and to suppress semantic nuances belonging to the individual evolution of each dialect: what remains is only an abstraction which is the means of justifying the relationship, but does not give us the original sense of the word. Looking through an etymological dictionary produces the illusion that the Indo-European language operated with words and roots which had

abstract and general meanings, while in fact one should rather think of each Indo-European language ... [as] ... poor in general terms but rich in specific terminology for particular activities and the details of familiar objects." I would not like to make Meillet's judgment about the poverty of Proto-Indo-European abstract vocabulary (though see Traugott's 1982 suggestions about historical accretion of abstract vocabulary). But the primacy and richness of basic-level concrete vocabulary remains a fact about any natural language, and Meillet's caution against relying on abstraction to give us proto-meanings of words is as cogent now as when it was written.

4 See for example, the work of Nagy (1974), Watkins, Jakobson, and others (references will be found in Nagy) on metrics; and of Watkins (1970, 1982, and elsewhere), Campanile (1974, 1982 and elsewhere), Durante (1958 and elsewhere), and others on metaphor and formulae.

5 Traugott's use of the terms *textual* and *expressive* is taken from Halliday and Hasan (1976). I prefer not to use these terms, as they do not precisely coincide with the sets of distinctions I am trying to make.

6 Some of this work (e.g. Traugott 1988) will be referred to later in this book.

7 My own past work since my dissertation (Sweetser 1986, 1987b, 1988) has continued to map out pieces of the lexicon and to try to further clarify the notion of "closeness" in given semantic areas, and the relationships between senses in those areas. Other recent work on the same issues includes that of Suzanne Fleischman (1989), Suzanne Kemmer (1988), Claudia Brugman (1983, 1984, 1988), and of course that of Traugott.

8 For those interested, the phonological history is as follows. The phrase *is samlaid* "it is likely/like" was given a new word-division as *is amlaid*, rather as Eng. *a napron* suffered reanalysis into *an apron*.

9 See various papers in Chafe and Nichols (1986), in particular Aksu-Koc and Slobin.

10 See Rogers (1971) on classes of perception verbs; also Ullmann's discussion of vision as the most "differentiated" of the senses (Ullmann 1962).

11 Orin Gensler carried out the Hebrew concordance search for me, and is very sincerely thanked for his help.

12 I have been unable to trace a science-fiction story I once read, which derived some humor from our understanding of this unique connection between tactile sense (as opposed to the others) and emotion. The hero is at one point tortured by aliens, who cannot believe his hardihood in being able to look unflinchingly on a particular shade of puce.

13 Jane Espenson (personal communication) has suggested to me that it is possible to see as consistent our two understandings of thought as travel and as possession/manipulation of objects, if we notice that physical locations (through which we travel) can themselves be seen as objects to be possessed or manipulated. For example, one can *hold onto* a position, or *abandon* it.

14 Vassiliki Nikiforidou and I are currently engaged in writing a study of structural parallelisms between semantic and phonological change, and in particular of regularity in the two domains, which treats these concerns in more detail.

3   Modality

1 An earlier and significantly different incarnation of this chapter appeared as Sweetser (1982), which is intended to be superseded by the present work.

2 I shall throughout the ensuing discussion refer to *root* modality, rather than using the term *deontic*. Not only is *root* a broader term (some might take *deontic* as indicative of purely social or moral obligation), but it also reflects my leaning towards an analysis of epistemic modal meaning as rooted in sociophysical (root) modality.

3 I personally have data showing that modal verbs have a root/epistemic ambiguity in both the Indo-European and Semitic language families at large, and also in Finnish and Tagalog. Tregidgo (1982) lists a much larger set of languages obtained by Perkins (forthcoming). I have not obtained a copy of Perkins' work, but the list is as follows: Basque, Classical Aztec, French, German, Italian, Kapampangan, Korean, Luiseño, Polish, Tamil, Thai, Tzeltal, Welsh, and "many ancient Indo-European languages." Palmer (1986), drawing on a much larger sample of languages, likewise agrees that there is a striking crosslinguistic tendency towards deontic and epistemic modal meanings being represented by the same vocabulary.

4 The morphology and syntax of the English modals is outside the scope of this work. I am, however, by no means the first to imagine that there is some connection between the semantic grouping of modal senses and the development of a morphologically and syntactically distinct set of modal verbs in English. Plank (1984) chides Lightfoot (1979) for ignoring the semantic unity of the modal verbs in his treatment of their historical-syntactic development.

5 There is a large literature on the subject of more and less prototypical agentivity and causality, which I cannot begin to discuss here. Shibatani (1976) (especially the paper by Talmy) is a valuable general reference. One other comment I have on the subject of more and less basic causality is that one could easily take the *let* of sentence (3) as being metaphorical, and claim that we understand non-intentional forces and barriers (like water and stones) in terms of our perceptually more basic concept of intentional force. This is what I feel is going on.

6 Viewing the schema of *may* as including a barrier, while *must* involves a force, also seems coherent with their different negation scopes. The negation of removing or holding back a barrier would be leaving it in place; hence *may not* becomes prohibition. *Must not*, on the other hand, is a very forceful prohibition, which is scarcely what one would expect if *must* is a barrier whose negation is an open path. Rather, the internal-negative reading of *must not* indicates an oppositely directed force, a force compelling that one *not* do whatever it is. Note that the external negation of a force would simply be the absence of the force, which is the reading we get for German *muss nicht*.

7 Robin Lakoff's (1973) rules of politeness have a bearing on this judgment: though as stated they do not directly forbid the giving of permission, her third

rule (which she labels "Equality/Camaraderie") directs the speaker to "make the interlocutor feel good – be friendly" – a goal best achieved by minimal exercise of overt authority. Her second maxim, "Give options," may also be relevant here; permission at least implicitly invokes the giver's ability to restrict the receiver's options.

8 Pp. 112ff.

9 The commonest use of *shall* in English is perhaps in consent requests for mutual action, like "Shall we dance?" In these questions, it is precisely our joint intent to *undertake* an action which is being queried; so my analysis seems to hold true for these examples as well. Likewise, in singular equivalents like "Shall I marry her?" (note the contrast with "Will I marry her?", the latter being a request for information about the future, while the former is a request for advice about undertaking a marriage), my undertaking to do so is in question. *Shall*-questions are so strongly linked with the speaker's undertaking that the third-person equivalents of these questions ("Shall he marry her?") still question the speaker's undertaking, rather than the subject's.

10 The term *distal* I have taken from Langacker (1978), who uses this term precisely to refer to a generic "distance" within either the temporal or the causal sequence. Palmer (1986) comments on the frequent use of tense marking to indicate distance from the speaker's viewpoint in modal systems. More recently, Fleischman (1989) has laid out in detail the multiple ways in which temporal *distance* is a metaphor for epistemic and social distance.

11 Lyons does not attempt to give a unified analysis based on this suggestion. The suggestion in fact appears at the end of his (separate) analyses of deontic and epistemic modality (pp. 843–845).

12 Boyd and Thorne, for example, analyze root *must* as "I state I (or some Pro) (Imp)," where *Imp* is an imperative predicate applied to the content of the sentence. Epistemic *must*, on the other hand, they take to be "I state," applied to the content of the sentence. There is a feature (*nec*), "necessary," which is marked on the predicate *Imp* in root-modal *must*, but on the predicate *state* in the epistemic *must*.

Tregidgo contrasts deontic and epistemic *must* as follows: the deontic "a must b" translates as "X DEMAND Y – Y CAUSE – ab," while the epistemic "a must b" will translate instead as "X DEMAND Y – Y STATE – ab."

13 Interestingly, Bybee (1988) and Bybee and Pagliuca (1985) have analyzed the contrast in the opposite direction, seeing the shift from root to epistemic senses as the loss of a specific parameter of connection of the modality with an agent. This is part of a broader understanding of grammaticalization as involving semantic abstraction and generalization. Sweetser (1988), in the same volume, should give some evidence of the major degree to which I share Bybee's general view of grammaticalization, and of some of my reasons for differing from her in this particular case, and holding to an understanding of a full metaphorical mapping rather than the loss of a feature.

14 Palmer (1986, pp. 11–12).

15 Palmer (1986, pp. 51ff., 70). Palmer contrasts these *judgmental* senses with

evidential senses which are more prominently featured in some other languages. I would argue that the English modals, particularly *must*, do sometimes show evidential-type uses; and indeed Palmer is probably correct in his suggestion that one cannot make a rigid division between evidential and judgmental.

16 The specific social use of *may* to indicate permission is later than the general sense of sociophysical potentiality or possibility, and presumably is a metonymic derivative of it; see Traugott (1988), and also my comments on Searle (1988) in section 3.3.3.

17 I would love to be able to explain why some of the root modals map better into the epistemic domain than others. *Shall* seems so much tied to the speaker that it is perhaps reasonable for it to lack an epistemic sense (there is no entity " the speaker" inside the epistemic world). But even that is just a guess. And why *can* and *need* should be epistemically used only in negative or interrogative forms, while *ought* has a full epistemic usage – perhaps the internality of *can* and *need* (while *ought* is social/external) makes them transfer less fully to epistemic use? But why do they transfer at all, then?

18 See von Wright (1951). This category is also used by Bybee (1985), Palmer (1986), and others.

19 Bybee (1985, p. 168) notes that what she calls *speaker-oriented* modalities, ones which are an expression of the speaker's attitude, are far more likely to be grammaticalized as part of verbal morphology than are *subject-oriented* modalities which are simply described by the speaker. Morphological abilitative markers do sometimes occur, as for example in the Philippine language family; I gather Bybee is saying they are much *rarer* than obligation-imposing modalities, such as hortatives or imperatives. It is an interesting fact that hortatives and imperatives (unlike their less morphologized cousins, lexical modal-verbs), are used pretty much exclusively, not just for *speaker-imposable* modalities, but for actual acts of imposing the relevant modality.

20 Bybee (1985) includes epistemic modalities among *speaker-oriented* modalities, noting that (like the performative uses of root modalities), epistemic-modal senses are very frequently grammaticalized in verb morphology.

21 I would like to thank Charles Fillmore for bringing this example to my attention.

22 I shall say more in chapter 4 about the use of *but* represented in these examples.

23 Compare the odd use of *perhaps* in (a) and (b):

(a) Perhaps he IS a professor; he's still a fool.
(b) Perhaps there IS a six-pack in the fridge; we have to get some work done.

This is parallel to the speech-act use of *if*-clauses (discussed in chapter 5), as exemplified in (c)–(d)

(c) (Even) if he IS a professor, he's dumb. (on a reading where I assume he's a professor)
(d) (Even) if there IS a six-pack in the fridge (as we know there is), we have to get some work done.

24 The literature on the root/epistemic distinction is strangely silent on the subject of these speech-act uses of modal verbs; nor do I know of any historical studies of their presence in English.

25 Examples like (40)–(43) were brought to my attention by Gilles Fauconnier. Another example which seems to resemble them, but may also resemble (36) and (37), is (a):

    (a) She *could* be the Pope, and I still wouldn't see her.

26 However, it may well be that these applications of modality to the form of the utterance, like metalinguistic uses of negation (see Horn 1985, cited in chapter 1), and like conditionality (discussed below in 5.4.3), should be treated independently as a separate category from speech-act modality uses.

27 Counterparts may exist in domains connected by other mappings than metaphorical ones. For example, a metonymic mapping between customers and foods ordered allows restaurant workers to refer to a customer using the name of the food (s)he ordered: "The ham sandwich is a lousy tipper."

4   Conjunction, coordination, and subordination

1 An earlier partial discussion of these causal-conjunction phenomena appears in Sweetser 1982.

2 In section 4.1.2, I shall discuss the presence of commas in (1b) and (1c), and the commalessness of (1a).

3 It is not impossible for content conjunction to occur in an imperative or interrogative speech-act, but such conjunction must be interpreted as *inside* the scope of the imperative or interrogative force. In cases like (1c), the conjunction is taken as *outside* the interrogative force, joining it to a separate assertive speech-act. See note 7 for a discussion of related issues.

4 *While*, interestingly, shows ambiguity between the epistemic and speech-act domains as a causal conjunction – (a) is epistemic and (b) is a speech-act conjunction:

    (a) *While* Paris is large, it is not impersonal.
        (Paris' largeness might lead me to *conclude* that it is impersonal, but despite this, other data lead me to a different conclusion.)
    (b) *While* I sympathize with your troubles, bring me a paper on Monday or else! (I *command* you despite my sympathy.)

However, in the content domain, *while* seems to have only its original sense of simple cotemporality. It is noteworthy (see Traugott 1982) to what an extent we draw on our lexicon of space and time to describe other relations such as causality and adversity.

5 Since writing the dissertation on which this book is based, I have discovered that Ducrot (1980, 1984) treats these contrasts between uses of French conjunctions in a way which interestingly parallels my analysis, at least insofar as he appeals to a speech-act context, rather than simply to content, in explaining the use of *puisque*. Examples of *parce que* and *puisque*:

(a) Il va l'épouser *parce qu'*il l'adore.
    "He's going to marry her because he adores her."
    (content reading: adoration causes engagement)
(b) (Mais si,) il va l'épouser, *puisqu'*il l'adore.
    "(But of course) he's going to marry her, since he adores her."
    (epistemic reading: we conclude the marriage is certain from our joint
    knowledge that he adores her)

6 Self-referential presupposition seems an inherently contradictory concept.

7 Conjunction is theoretically a relationship between *clauses*, not between
   utterances. My claim is that conjunction between clauses in interpreted in (at
   least) three major distinct ways relative to the content of the clauses. It is
   interesting to note the approach of earlier work (see Ross 1967; Emonds 1970)
   to the problems of conjunction and subordination. Ross is concerned that the
   same transformations must apply (Across-the-Board) to all conjuncts of a
   conjoined structure; Emonds is trying to account for the fact that
   transformations like Subj-Aux Inversion only apply in Root clauses (or, of
   course, across the board in conjuncts immediately subjacent to a Root clause).
   Examples like (1c) or (27)–(30) do not fit either set of generalizations; precisely
   when conjunction of clauses is intended to conjoin speech acts, the conjoined
   clauses behave as syntactically independent. This is because they are linked not
   at the syntactic but at the pragmatic level. Ross' and Edmonds' theories do not
   account for such an interpretation of conjunction, nor for the accompanying
   syntactic behavior.

8 For further discussion of the distinction between polysemy and pragmatically
   distinct uses of an abstract sense, see Sweetser (1986).

9 In fact, the bizarreness of an abstract syntactic analysis would be increased by
   the addition of epistemic, as well as speech-act, higher predicates.

10 A logical-conjunction analysis of *and* requires that it conjoin only propositions
   at the semantic level (sentences, at the syntactic level). But for natural
   language, there seems to be every reason to doubt that *and*'s semantic behavior
   is limited to proposition joining. (See note 7.)

11 Suppose that one could systematically differentiate in some way between
   oppositions such as *rich* vs. *poor* and oppositions such as *Catholic* vs. *socialist*.
   One might label the former genuine semantic oppositions, meaning that the
   semantic content of the contrasted expressions involves opposed features such
   as A and ∼ A. The latter group might rather be labeled "pragmatic
   oppositions," meaning that the actual semantics of the two expressions are not
   in opposition, but rather the pragmatic framings of those semantic structures
   are contrasted. One would then be able to make a case for the treatment of *but*
   in (56) as content-conjoining. The major difficulty, it seems to me, would be
   to systematically differentiate between the two kinds of oppositions. A linguist
   who wished to make *all* of these oppositions semantic might just include in an
   analysis of *socialist* the feature [− religious]; we would not want to allow such
   essentially *ad-hoc* manipulation of the semantics–pragmatics borderline.
   Further, all of recent work in cognitive semantics has tended to confirm that
   contextual framing is not readily separable from an autonomous level of

lexical-semantic meaning, but that it is an inextricably interwoven part of meaning-structure. If this is so, the attempted differentiation between the *rich/poor* contrast and the *Catholic/socialist* one may be predestined to failure in any case.

12 The speech-act use of *but* in example (37) in chapter 3 ("There may be a six-pack in the fridge, but we have work to do") might be similarly analyzed: if I am willing to agree that "there's a six-pack in the fridge," perhaps my interlocutor might expect me to go on to accept the offer conveyed by this statement. But (37) is a refusal of the offer.

13 It has been shown by G. Lakoff (1986) that the aberrance or naturalness of event-sequences affects the interaction of syntactic rules with the syntax of the clauses used to represent those event-sequences; in particular, the Coordinate Structure Constraint (see Ross 1967 [1986]) can be explained largely in terms of the pragmatic assumptions of natural and unnatural sequences of events.

14 See R. Lakoff (1971, pp. 137ff.).

15 Two separate lines of reasoning seem to be involved in the presupposition that the criminal's capture would be normal, versus the idea that escape is normal. The idea that an unjust situation is normally followed by a reassertion of justice would lead us to expect the capture; the idea that somehow injustices proliferate (once started) would lead us to expect the escape.

16 Note the strong counterfactual force of *would* when followed by *but*; a following *but* adds to the dubitativity of *could* and *should* as well.

17 Direct statements are generally more independent than presuppositions – and hence presuppositions are cancellable, while direct statements are not.

5   Conditionals

1 I shall also primarily be looking at particular ways in which one and the same conditional-sentence form may have different interpretations, rather than at the way in which certain parts of a conditional sentence's form (e.g. verb tenses) may vary and thus regularly convey different meanings or speech-act forces. For a recent examination of the different formal-construction varieties of conditionals, see Fillmore (1986).

2 By "sufficient," I mean sufficient in the real-world sense; e.g., the event described in the protasis might be a sufficient *cause* for the event described in the apodosis. I do not mean "sufficient" as in the logician's "(necessary and) sufficient."

3 It is not normal for a speaker to make dubitative statements about his/her own present or recent past – areas where the adult, conscious speaker is presumably the primary authority. Hence (5) necessarily presumes the speaker not to be president.

4 Note the way in which, as with modals, a past-tense verb form significantly raises the plausibility of an epistemic reading in (7). Presumably we tend to think it more likely that a thinker's reasoning processes concerning past events should be undetermined and conditional than that the past events themselves should be so.

5 Conversationally, these speech-act conditionals can be regarded as a self-protection mechanism on the speaker's part – a way of saying possibly inappropriate things, while nonetheless insuring against potential reproof or responsibility by merely saying these things *conditionally*. In this sense, the use of speech-act conditionals parallels the use of certain self-excusing expressions which are often used to guard against potential criticism (see Baker 1975). It is harder to make a direct criticism of a speaker who has already self-critically made excuses for the fault in question.

6 We may call this excluded reading a "questioned conditional"; my focus throughout this work is rather on "conditional questions" as one instance of the more general category of conditional speech-acts. The difference is clearly conveyed by the following formulae:
   Questioned conditional: Q (IF[x] THEN[y])
   Conditional question: IF(x) THEN Q(y)

7 For a somewhat different perspective on conditional speech acts, see my discussion of Van der Auwera (1986) in the appendix to this chapter.

8 Haiman's analysis might be taken as fitting in well with interpretations of conditionality as involving a "speech act of supposing" – e.g. Mackie (1973) (quoted in Van der Auwera 1986), or Ducrot (1972).

9 Dancygier (1987) discusses the ways in which certain kinds of conditionals evoke the speaker's knowledge or the supposedly shared knowledge of speaker and hearer; her categorization, as she states, in some ways parallels my speech-act and epistemic-conditional categories.

10 From Jespersen (1940, p. 378); discussed in Haiman (1978). Jespersen terms this a "pseudo-condition." The interested reader can look up the quote itself in Defoe's *Robinson Crusoe*, p. 149 [Modern Library edition].

11 I would like to thank Barbara Dancygier for sharing her work with me, not only in written form, but in some extremely enlightening discussions.

12 Seemingly "fake" conditionals such as "She's forty if she's a day" could presumably also be analyzed as "given" conditions. The proposition "she's forty" is treated as being so obviously true that it is conditional only on the ridiculously over-obvious proposition that "she's (at least) a day (old)."

13 "Clausal topic" means "a clause which is the topic of an utterance," and *not* "the topic of a clause."

14 Fauconnier analyzes the inherent scalar phenomena involved in various English logical operators and lexemes. More recently, analyses of the semantics of *even* and of the English *let alone* construction (as in *Sally won't eat shrimp, let alone squid*) have been published, which make use of the notion of pragmatic scale as a crucial component in the semantics of these English words and constructions. (See Kay 1987; Fillmore, Kay, and O'Connor 1988.)

6   Retrospect and prospect

1 See Sweetser (1988) for further arguments to this effect.

2 See Givón 1973; Fleischman 1982a, b; Kemmer 1988; Genetti 1986; Sweetser 1988; Traugott 1982, 1988; and many others.

References

Akmajian, Adrian 1984. Sentence types and the form–function fit. *Natural Language and Linguistic Theory 1*: 2, pp. 1–23.

Aksu-Koc, Ayhan A., and Dan I. Slobin 1986. A psychological account of the development and use of evidentials in Turkish. In Chafe and Nichols (eds.), pp. 159–167.

Antinucci, Francesco and Domenico Parisi 1971. On English modal verbs. *CLS 7*, pp. 28–39.

Austin, J. L. 1961. Ifs and cans. In J. L. Austin, *Philosophical papers*, ed. J. O. Urmson and G. J. Warnock (3rd edition, 1979). Oxford: Oxford University Press, pp. 153–180.

1962. *How to do things with words*. Cambridge, MA: Harvard University Press.

Baker, Charlotte 1975. This is just a first approximation, but... *CLS 11*, pp. 37–47.

Basilius, Harold 1952. Neo-Humboldtian ethnolinguistics. *Word 8*, pp. 95–105.

Bates, Elizabeth, Luigia Camaioni, and Virginia Volterra 1979. The acquisition of performatives prior to speech. In Ochs and Schieffelin (eds.), pp. 111–130.

Benveniste, Emile 1969. *Le vocabulaire des institutions indo-européennes* (2 volumes). Paris: Minuit.

1971. Semantic problems in reconstruction. In *Problems in general linguistics*. Coral Gables: University of Miami Press, pp. 249–264.

Berlin, Brent and Paul Kay 1969. *Basic color terms: their universality and evolution*. Berkeley: University of California Press.

Bloom, Lois and Joanne Bitetti Capatides 1987. Sources of meaning in the acquisition of complex syntax: the sample case of causality. *Journal of Experimental Child Psychology 43*, pp. 112–128.

Bolinger, Dwight 1965. The atomization of meaning. *Language 41*, pp. 555–573.

1977. *Meaning and form*. London: Longman.

Boyd, Julian and J. P. Thorne 1969. The semantics of modal verbs. *Journal of Linguistics 5*, pp. 57–74.

Brugman, Claudia M. 1983. The use of body-part terms as locatives in Chalcotongo Mixtec. In *Report no. 4 from the Survey of California and Other Indian Languages*. Published by the Survey of California and Other Indian Languages at the University of California at Berkeley.

1984. The *very* idea: a case study in polysemy and cross-lexical generalizations. In *Papers from the parasession on lexical semantics*. Chicago: Chicago Linguistic Society, pp. 21–38.

1988. *The story of* over: *polysemy, semantics, and the structure of the lexicon.*
New York: Garland.

Brugman, Claudia M. and George Lakoff (in press). Cognitive topology and
lexical networks. In G. Cottrell, S. Small, and M. K. Tanenhaus (eds.)
Lexical ambiguity resolution. Palo Alto, CA: Morgan Kaufmann, pp.
477–508.

Buck, Carl Darling 1949. *A dictionary of selected synonyms in the principal Indo-
European languages.* Chicago: University of Chicago Press.

Bybee, Joan L. 1985. *Morphology: a study of the relation between meaning and
form.* Amsterdam: John Benjamins.

1988. Semantic substance vs. contrast in the development of grammatical
meaning. In Shelley Axmaker, Annie Jaisser, and Helen Singmaster (eds.)
*Proceedings of the fourteenth annual meeting of the Berkeley Linguistics
Society,* pp. 247–279. Berkeley, CA: Berkeley Linguistic Society.

Bybee, Joan L., and William Pagliuca 1985. Cross-linguistic comparison and the
development of grammatical meaning. In J. Fisiak (ed.) *Historical semantics
and historical word-formation.* Berlin: Mouton, pp. 59–84.

Campanile, Enrico 1974. Indo-European metaphors and non-Indo-European
metaphors. *Journal of Indo-European Studies 2,* pp. 247–258.

1982. Sulla preistoria di Lat. *pontifex. Studi classici e orientali XXXII,* pp.
291–297.

Chafe, Wallace L. 1984. How people use adverbial clauses. *BLS 10,* pp. 437–
449.

Chafe, Wallace L., and Johanna Nichols (eds.) 1986. *Evidentiality: the linguistic
coding of epistemology.* Norwood, NJ: Ablex.

Chantraine, Pierre. 1968–1980. *Dictionnaire étymologique de la langue grecque:
histoire des mots* (4 volumes). Paris: Klincksieck.

Clark, Eve V. 1976. Universal categories: on the semantics of classifiers and
children's early word meanings. In Alphonse Juilland (ed.) *Linguistic studies
offered to Joseph Greenberg (Studia Linguistica et Philologica 4:3).* Saratoga,
CA: Anma Libri. Vol. 3, pp. 449–462.

Clark, Herbert 1973. Space, time, semantics, and the child. In T. Moore (ed.)
Cognitive development and the acquisition of language. New York: Academic
Press, pp. 27–63.

Coleman, Linda and Paul Kay 1981. Prototype semantics: the English word *lie.*
Language 57, pp. 26–44.

Comrie, Bernard 1986. Conditionals: a typology. In E. C. Traugott, A. ter
Meulen, J. Snitzer Reilly, and C. A. Ferguson (eds.), Cambridge: Cambridge
University Press, pp. 77–102.

Dancygier, Barbara 1987. Conditionals and relevance. Paper presented at the 1987
International Pragmatics Conference in Antwerp.

forthcoming. Two metalinguistic operators in English and Polish.

Davison, Alice 1973. Performative verbs, adverbs and felicity conditions: an
inquiry into the nature of performative verbs. Unpublished PhD dissertation,
University of Chicago.

Dowty, David R. 1979. *Word meaning and Montague grammar*. Dordrecht: Reidel.

Ducrot, Oswald 1972. *Dire et ne pas dire: principes de sémantique linguistique*. Paris: Hermann.

1980. *Les mots du discours*. Paris: Minuit.

1984. *Le dire et le dit*. Paris: Minuit.

Durante, Marcello 1958. Epea pteroenta. La Parole come "cammino" in imagine greche e vediche. *Atti della Accademia Nazionale dei Lincei, Anno CCLV. Classe di Scienze morali, storiche e filologiche, 13*, pp. 3–14.

Ehrman, Madeline E. 1966. *The meanings of the modals in present-day American English*. (Series Practica 45) The Hague: Mouton.

Emonds, Joseph 1970. Root and structure-preserving transformations. Unpublished PhD dissertation, MIT.

Ernout, Alfred and Antoine Meillet 1959. *Dictionnaire étymologique de la langue latine: histoire des mots*. (4th edition) Paris: Klincksieck.

Ernst, Thomas B. 1984. Towards an integrated theory of adverb position in English. Unpublished Ph.D. dissertation, distributed by Indiana University Linguistics Club.

Fauconnier, Gilles 1975. Pragmatic scales and logical structures. *Linguistic Inquiry 6*, pp. 353–375.

1985. *Mental spaces: roles and strategies*. Cambridge, MA: MIT Press.

Fillmore, Charles J. 1971. *The Santa Cruz lectures on deixis*. Bloomington, IN: Indiana University Linguistics Club.

1976. Frame semantics and the nature of language. In Stevan R. Harnad, H. D. Steklis, and J. Lancaster (eds.) *Origins and evolution of language and speech*. New York: New York Academy of Sciences, pp. 20–32.

1977. Topics in lexical semantics. In Roger W. Cole (ed.) *Current issues in linguistic theory*. Bloomington: Indiana University Press, pp. 76–138.

1982. Towards a descriptive framework for spatial deixis. In Robert J. Jarvella and Wolfgang Klein (eds.) *Speech, place, and action: studies in deixis and related topics*. Chichester and New York: John Wiley and Sons, pp. 31–59.

1985. Frames and the semantics of understanding. *Quaderni di Semantica 6: 2*, pp. 222–254.

1986. Varieties of conditional sentences. *Eastern States Conference on Linguistics 6*.

Fillmore, Charles J., Paul Kay, and M. Catherine O'Connor 1988. Regularity and idiomaticity in grammatical constructions: the case of *let alone*. *Language 64:3*, pp. 501–538.

Fleischman, Suzanne 1982a. *The future in thought and language: diachronic evidence from Romance*. Cambridge: Cambridge University Press.

1982b. The past and the future: are they *coming* or *going*? In M. Macaulay, O. Gensler, *et al.* (eds.) *Proceedings of the eighth annual meeting of the Berkeley Linguistics Society*, pp. 322–334.

1983. From pragmatics to grammar: diachronic reflections on complex pasts and futures in Romance. *Lingua 60*, pp. 183–214.

1989. Temporal distance. *Studies in Language 13:1*, pp. 1–51.

Friedrich, Paul 1979. Proto-Indo-European trees. In *Language, context, and the imagination.* Stanford University Press, pp. 251–289.

Gazdar, Gerald 1979. *Pragmatics: implicature, presupposition, and logical form.* New York: Academic Press.

Gazdar, Gerald, Ewan Klein, Geoffrey Pullum, and Ivan Sag 1985. *Generalized phrase structure grammar.* Cambridge, MA: Harvard University Press.

Genetti, Carol 1986. The development of subordinators from postpositions in Bodic languages. *BLS 12*, pp. 387–400.

Gentner, Dedre and Donald R. Gentner 1982. Flowing waters or teeming crowds: mental models of electricity. Report no. 4981, prepared for the Office of Naval Research Personnel and Training Research Programs. Boston: Bolt Beranek and Newman Inc.

Givón, Talmy 1973. The time-axis phenomenon. *Language 49*, pp. 890–925.

Gordon, David and George Lakoff 1971. Conversational postulates. *CLS 7*, pp. 63–84.

Grice, H. P. 1975. Logic and conversation. In Peter Cole and Jerry Morgan (eds.) *Syntax and semantics, Vol. 3: Speech acts.* New York: Academic Press, pp. 41–58.

1978. Further notes on logic and conversation. In Peter Cole (ed.) *Syntax and semantics, Vol. 9: Pragmatics.* New York: Academic Press, pp. 113–127.

Gumperz, John J. 1982. *Discourse strategies.* Cambridge: Cambridge University Press.

Haiman, John 1978. Conditionals are topics. *Language 54*, pp. 564–589.

1980. The iconicity of grammar: isomorphism and motivation. *Language 56*, pp. 515–540.

1986. Constraints on the form and meaning of the protasis. In E. C. Traugott, A. ter Meulen, J. Snitzer Reilly, and C. A. Ferguson (eds.) *On conditionals.* Cambridge: Cambridge University Press, pp. 215–228.

Halliday, M. A. K. and Ruqaiya Hasan 1976. *Cohesion in English.* London: Longman.

Hock, Hans Henrich 1986. *Principles of historical linquistics.* Berlin: Mouton de Gruyter.

Holdcroft, David 1971. Conditional assertion. *Proceedings of the Aristotelian Society, supplementary volume 45*, pp. 123–139.

Horn, Laurence R. 1972. *On the semantic properties of logical operators in English.* PhD dissertation, UCLA. Published by Indiana University Linguistics Club.

1985. Metalinguistic negation and pragmatic ambiguity. *Language 61:1*, pp. 121–174.

Huddleston, Rodney 1979. *Would have become*: empty or modal *will*. *Journal of Linguistics 15*, pp. 335–340.

Jackendoff, Ray 1972. *Semantic interpretation in generative grammar.* Cambridge, MA: MIT Press.

1983. *Semantics and cognition.* Cambridge, MA: MIT Press.

Jespersen, Otto 1940. *A modern English grammar on historical principles, Vol. V: Syntax*. London: George Allen and Unwin.
  1964. *Essentials of English grammar*. University, Alabama: University of Alabama Press.
Johnson, Mark 1987. *The body in the mind*. Chicago: University of Chicago Press.
Katz, Jerrold J. and Jerry A. Fodor 1963. The structure of a semantic theory. *Language 39*, pp. 170–210.
Kay, Paul 1983. Linguistic competence and folk theories of language: two English hedges. *BLS 9*, pp. 128–137.
Kay, Paul, and Chad K. MacDaniel 1978. The linguistic significance of the meanings of basic level color terms. *Language 54*, pp. 610–646.
Kay, Paul, and Willett Kempton 1984. What is the Sapir–Whorf hypothesis? *American Anthropologist 86:1*, pp. 65–79.
Kemmer, Suzanne 1988. The middle voice: a typological and diachronic study. Unpublished PhD dissertation, Stanford University.
Kiparsky, Paul 1968. Linguistic universals and linguistic change. In E. Bach and R. T. Harms (eds.) *Universals in Linguistic Theory*. New York: Holt, Rinehart and Winston, pp. 170–210.
Kratzer, Angelika 1977. What "must" and "can" must and can mean. *Linguistics and Philosophy 1*, pp. 337–355.
Kuczaj, Stan A. (II) and Mary J. Daly 1979. The development of hypothetical reference in the speech of young children. *Journal of Child Language 6*, pp. 563–579.
Kurath, Hans 1921. *The semantic sources of the words for the emotions in Sanskrit, Greek, Latin, and the Germanic languages*. PhD dissertation, University of Chicago. Published by The Collegiate Press, George Banta Publishing Co., Menasha, Wisconsin.
Lakoff, George 1972. Hedges: a study in meaning criteria and the logic of fuzzy concepts. *CLS 8*, pp. 183–228.
  1986. Frame-semantic control of the coordinate structure constraint. *CLS 22*, pp. 152–167.
  1987. *Women, fire, and dangerous things: what categories reveal about the mind*. Chicago: University of Chicago Press.
Lakoff, George, and Mark Johnson 1980. *Metaphors we live by*. Chicago: University of Chicago Press.
Lakoff, Robin T. 1971. If's, and's, and but's about conjunction. In Charles J. Fillmore and D. Terence Langendoen (eds.) *Studies in linguistic semantics*. New York: Holt, Rinehart and Winston, pp. 114–149.
  1972a. The pragmatics of modality. *CLS 8*, pp. 229–246.
  1972b. Language in context. *Language 48*, pp. 907–927.
  1973. The logic of politeness; or, minding your p's and q's. *CLS 9*, pp. 292–305.
Langacker, Ronald 1978. The form and meaning of the English auxiliary. *Language 54*, pp. 853–882.
Lewis D. 1975. Causation. In Sosa (ed.), pp. 180–191.

164   *References*

Lightfoot, David W. 1979. *Principles of diachronic syntax.* Cambridge: Cambridge University Press.
Lindner, Susan Jean 1981. *A lexico-semantic analysis of English verb particle constructions with "out" and "up."* PhD dissertation, University of California, San Diego. Published by Indiana University Linguistics Club.
Lounsbury, Floyd G. 1964. The structural analysis of kinship semantics. In Horace G. Lunt (ed.) *Proceedings of the ninth International Congress of Linguists.* The Hague: Mouton, pp. 1073–1093.
Lyons, John 1977. *Semantics* (2 volumes). Cambridge: Cambridge University Press.
Mackie, John Leslie 1973. *Truth, probability, and paradox: studies in philosophical logic.* Oxford: Oxford University Press.
Matisoff, James A. 1978. *Variational semantics in Tibeto-Burman: the "organic" approach to linguistic comparison.* Philadelphia: Institute for the Study of Human Issues.
Meillet, Antoine 1937 [1964]. *Introduction à l'étude comparative des langues indo-européennes.* 8th edn, reprinted (1964) by University of Alabama Press.
Mervis, Carolyn B. and Eleanor Rosch 1981. Categorization of natural objects. *Annual Review of Psychology 32*, pp. 89–115.
Mithun, Marianne 1980. A functional approach to syntactic reconstruction. In Elizabeth C. Traugott, Rebecca LaBrum, and Susan Shepherd (eds.) *Papers from the fourth International Conference on Historical Linguistics.* Amsterdam: Benjamins, pp. 87–96.
Nagy, Gregory 1974. *Comparative studies in Greek and Indic meter.* Cambridge, MA: Harvard University Press.
Ochs, Elinor and Bambi B. Schieffelin 1979. *Developmental pragmatics.* New York: Academic Press.
Öhman, Suzanne 1953. Theories of the "linguistic field." *Word 9*, pp. 123–134.
Osgood, Charles E., George J. Suci, and Percy H. Tannenbaum 1957. *The measurement of meaning.* Urbana: University of Illinois Press.
Osgood, Charles E., William H. May, and Murray S. Miron 1975. *Crosscultural universals of affective meaning.* Urbana: University of Illinois Press.
Palmer, Frank Robert 1979. *Modality and the English modals.* London: Longman.
  1986. *Mood and modality.* Cambridge: Cambridge University Press.
Perkins, M. R. forthcoming. The atomic structure of the English modals (cited in Tregidgo 1982).
Plank, Frans 1984. The modals story retold. *Studies in Language 8:3*, pp. 305–364.
Pokorny, Julius 1959–1969. *Indogermanisches etymologisches Wörterbuch* (2 volumes). Bern and Munich: Francke Verlag.
Ransom, Evelyn N. 1977. On the representation of modality. *Linguistics and Philosophy 1*, pp. 357–379.
Rappaport, Gilbert 1980. Deixis and detachment in the adverbial participles of Russian. In Catherine V. Chvany and Richard D. Brecht (eds.) *Morphosyntax in Slavic.* Columbus, OH: Slavica Publishers, pp. 273–300.
Reddy, Michael 1979. The conduit metaphor. In A. Ortony (ed.) *Metaphor and thought.* Cambridge: Cambridge University Press.

Rogers, Andy 1971. Three kinds of physical perception verbs. *CLS 7*, pp. 206–222.

Rosch, Eleanor H. 1973. Natural categories. *Cognitive Psychology 4*, pp. 328–350.

1977. Human categorization. In Neil Warren (ed.) *Studies in cross-cultural psychology, Volume 1*. London: Academic Press, pp. 1–49.

1978. Principles of categorization. In E. Rosch and B. B. Lloyd (eds.) *Cognition and categorization*. Hillsdale, NJ: Erlbaum, pp. 27–48.

Ross, John Robert 1967 [1986]. *Constraints on variables in syntax*. PhD dissertation, MIT. Published by Indiana University Linguistics Club. (Now reprinted as *Infinite Syntax*. Norwood, NJ: Ablex.)

1970. On declarative sentences. In Roderick A. Jacobs and Peter S. Rosenbaum (eds.) *Readings in English transformational grammar*. Waltham, MA: Ginn and Co., pp. 222–272.

Sapir, Edward 1921. *Language*. New York: Harcourt, Brace, and World.

1949 [1929]. The status of linguistics as a science. In David Mandelbaum (ed.) *Selected writings of Edward Sapir*. Berkeley and Los Angeles, CA: University of California Press. (Originally published in *Language 5*, pp. 207–214.)

Saussure, Ferdinand de 1959 [1915]. *Course in general linguistics*, eds. Charles Bally and Albert Sechehaye; trans. Wade Baskin. New York: Philosophical Library.

Schank, Roger C. and R. P. Abelson 1977. *Scripts, plans, goals, and understanding: an inquiry into human knowledge structures*. Hillsdale, NJ: Lawrence Erlbaum.

Searle, John R. 1969. *Speech acts: an essay in the philosophy of language*. Cambridge: Cambridge University Press.

1979. *Expression and meaning* . Cambridge: Cambridge University Press.

1983. *On intentionality*. Cambridge: Cambridge University Press.

in press. How performatives work. *Linguistics and Philosophy*.

Shepherd, Susan C. 1981. Modals in Antiguan Creole, child language acquisition, and history. Unpublished PhD dissertation, Stanford University.

1982. From deontic to epistemic: an analysis of modals in the history of English, creoles, and language acquisition. In A. Ahlqvist (ed.) *Papers from the fifth International Conference on Historical Linguistics*. Amsterdam: John Benjamins, pp. 316–323.

Shibatani, Masayoshi (ed.) 1976. *Syntax and semantics, Vol. 6: The grammar of causative constructions*. New York: Academic Press.

Slobin, Dan I. 1973. Cognitive prerequisites for the development of grammar. In Charles A. Ferguson and Dan Isaac Slobin (eds.) *Studies of child language development*. New York: Holt, Rinehart and Winston, pp. 175–276.

Sosa, Ernest (ed.) 1975. *Causation and conditionals*. Oxford Readings in Philosophy. Oxford: Oxford University Press.

Stalnaker, Robert C. 1968. A theory of conditionals. In Nicholas Rescher (ed.) *Studies in logical theory*. Oxford: Blackwell. *American Philosophical Quarterly, Monograph Series* no. 2, pp. 98–112. (Reprinted in Sosa (ed.), pp. 165–179.)

Stern, Gustav 1931. *Meaning and change of meaning*. Bloomington: Indiana University Press.

Sweetser, Eve E. 1982. Root and epistemic modals: causality in two worlds. In M. Macaulay, O. Gensler, *et al.* (eds.) *Proceedings of the eighth annual meeting of the Berkeley Linguistics Society.* Berkeley, CA: Berkeley Linguistics Society, pp. 484–507.

1984a. Semantic structure and semantic change: English perception-verbs in an Indo-European context. Distributed by the Linguistics Agency of the University of Trier (LAUT); now distributed by the Linguistics Agency of the University of Duisburg.

1984b. Semantic structure and semantic change: a cognitive linguistic study of modality, perception, speech acts, and logical relations. PhD dissertation, University of California at Berkeley. Ann Arbor: University Microfilms.

1986. Polysemy vs abstraction: mutually exclusive or complementary? In D. Feder, M. Niepokuj, V. Nikiforidou, and M. Van Clay (eds.) *Proceedings of the twelfth annual meeting of the Berkeley Linguistics Society.* Berkeley, CA: Berkeley Linguistics Society, pp. 528–538.

1987a. The definition of *lie*: an examination of the folk theories underlying a semantic prototype. In Dorothy Holland and Naomi Quinn (eds.) *Cultural models in language and thought.* Cambridge: Cambridge University Press, pp. 43–66.

1987b. Metaphorical models of thought and speech: a comparison of historical directions and metaphorical mappings in the two domains. In Jon Aske, Natasha Beery, Laura Michaelis, and Hana Filip (eds.) *Proceedings of the thirteenth annual meeting of the Berkeley Linguistics Society.* Berkeley, CA: Berkeley Linguistics Society, pp. 446–459.

1988. Grammaticalization and semantic bleaching. In Shelley Axmaker, Annie Jaisser, and Helen Singmaster (eds.) *Proceedings of the fourteenth annual meeting of the Berkeley Linguistics Society.* Berkeley, CA: Berkeley Linguistics Society, pp. 389–405.

Szemerenyi, Oswald 1962. Principles of etymological research in the Indo-European languages. In *Fachtagung für indogermanische und allgemeine Sprachwissenschaft.* Innsbrucker Beiträge zur Kulturwissenschaft, Sonderheft 15, II, pp. 175–212.

Talmy, Leonard 1976. Semantic causative types. In Shibatani (ed.), pp. 43–116.

1981. Force dynamics. Paper presented at the conference on Language and Mental Imagery, May 1981, University of California at Berkeley.

1988. Force dynamics in language and cognition. *Cognitive Science 2*, pp. 49–100.

Traugott, Elizabeth Closs 1974. Explorations in linguistic elaboration; language change, language acquisition, and the genesis of spatio-temporal terms. In John M. Anderson and Charles Jones (eds.) *Historical linguistics I.* Amsterdam: North Holland, pp. 263–314.

1982. From propositional to textual and expressive meanings: some semantic–pragmatic aspects of grammaticalization. In Winfred P. Lehmann and Yakov Malkiel (eds.) *Perspectives on historical linguistics.* Amsterdam: Benjamins, pp. 245–271.

1985. Conditional markers. In John Haiman (ed.) *Iconicity in syntax.* Amsterdam: Benjamins, pp. 289–310.

1986. From polysemy to internal semantic reconstruction. In D. Feder, M. Niepokuj, V. Nikiforidou, and M. Van Clay (eds.) *Proceedings of the twelfth annual meeting of the Berkeley Linguistics Society*, pp. 539–550.

1987. From less to more situated in language: the unidirectionality of semantic change. Paper given at the fifth International Conference on English Historical Linguistics, Cambridge, England.

1988. Pragmatic strengthening and grammaticalization. In Shelley Axmaker, Annie Jaisser, and Helen Singmaster (eds.), *Proceedings of the fourteenth annual meeting of the Berkeley Linguistics Society*, pp. 406–416.

1989. On the rise of epistemic meanings in English: an example of subjectification in semantic change. *Language 65: 1*, pp. 31–55.

in press. English speech act verbs: a historical perspective. To appear in Linda R. Waugh (ed.) *New vistas in grammar: invariance and variation.*

Tregidgo, P. S. 1982. MUST and MAY: demand and permission. *Lingua 56*, pp. 75–92.

Turner, Mark 1987. *Death is the mother of beauty.* Chicago, IL: University of Chicago Press.

Ullmann, Stephen 1962. *Semantics: an introduction to the science of meaning.* Oxford: Basil Blackwell.

Van der Auwera, Johan 1986. Conditionals and speech acts. In E. C. Traugott, A. ter Meulen, J. Snitzer Reilly, and C. A. Ferguson (eds.) *On Conditionals.* Cambridge: Cambridge University Press, pp 197–214.

Vendler, Zeno 1967. *Linguistics in philosophy.* Ithaca, NY: Cornell University Press.

Volterra, Virginia and Francesco Antinucci 1979. Negation in child language: a pragmatic study. In Ochs and Schieffelin (eds.), pp. 281–304.

von Wright, G. H. 1951. *An essay in modal logic.* Amsterdam: North Holland.

1975. On the logic and epistemology of the causal relation. In Sosa (ed.), pp. 95–113.

Watkins, Calvert 1970. Language of gods and language of men: remarks on some Indo-European metalinguistic traditions. In J. Puhvel (ed.) *Myth and law among the Indo-Europeans.* Berkeley: University of California Press, pp. 1–17.

1982. Aspects of Indo-European poetics. In Edgar Polomé (ed.) *The Indo-Europeans in the fourth and third millennia.* Ann Arbor: Karoma Publishers, Inc., pp. 100–121.

Wierzbicka, Anna 1980. *Lingua mentalis: the semantics of natural language.* Sydney and New York: Academic Press.

Whorf, Benjamin L. 1956a [1940]. Science and linguistics. In John B. Carroll (ed.) *Language, thought, and reality.* Cambridge MA: MIT Press, pp. 207–219 (Originally published in *Technology Review 42*, pp. 229–231, 247–248.)

1956b [1941]. The relation of habitual thought and behavior to language. In John B. Carroll (ed.) *Language, thought, and reality.* Cambridge MA: MIT Press, pp. 134–159. (Originally published in Leslie Spier (ed.) *Language, culture, and personality: essays in memory of Edward Sapir.* Menasha, Wisconsin: Sapir Memorial Publications Fund, pp. 75–93.)

Index of names

Subject index

174 Subject index

.